UNDERSTANDING STUDENT TEACHING

Case Studies of Experiences and Suggestions for Survival

EGERTON O. OSUNDE

Bloomsburg University of Pennsylvania

University Press of America, Inc.
Lanham • New York • Oxford

Copyright © 1999 by
University Press of America,® Inc.
4720 Boston Way
Lanham, Maryland 20706

12 Hid's Copse Rd.
Cumnor Hill, Oxford OX2 9JJ

Library of Congress Cataloging-in-Publication Data

Osunde, Egerton Oyenmwense.
Understanding student teaching : case studies of experiences and
suggestions for survival / Egerton O. Osunde.
p.   cm.
Includes bibliographical references and index.
1. Student teaching—United States Case Studies. I. Title.
LB2157.U5078   1999   370'.71—dc21   99—41525 CIP

ISBN 0-7618-1498-1 (cloth: alk. ppr.)
ISBN 0-7618-1499-X (pbk: alk. ppr.)

The paper used in this publication meets the minimum
requirements of American National Standard for Information
Sciences—Permanence of Paper for Printed Library Materials,
ANSI Z39.48—1984

Dedicated to my student teachers
and my children

Contents

Foreword

The *National Education Goals for the Year 2000* proposed the improvement of education as a major goal if the United States is to remain competitive in the global economy. Since the launching of this education reform initiative in 1989 by President George Bush, the Department of Education, at both the national and state levels, and school districts and universities have been working for the attainment of excellence in public education. Recent publications by the Carnegie Foundation (1986), *A Nation Prepared: Teachers for the 21st Century;* the Holmes Group Report (1986), *Tomorrow's Teachers;* and the Council for Basic Education (1996), *What Teachers Have to Say About Teacher Education,* advocate changes in teacher education as a way to enhance public education. As a result of these reports, colleges of education and their faculty have been seeking ways to strengthen the academic and professional development of teachers.

This book helps to provide student teachers with the knowledge and skills needed to become effective in the classroom and the teaching profession. The book also seeks to simplify the task of all those who work with student teachers and should be particularly helpful for cooperating teachers and college supervisors.

Dr. Osunde uses case studies to illustrate common classroom problems and show how student teachers have handled them. He goes on to provide theoretical suggestions and guidelines on how these challenges can be addressed. I am impressed that the book includes a chapter on teaching in an inclusive and culturally diverse classroom. In addition, the author addresses the question of ethics. Dr. Osunde maintains that many student teachers do not know what is professionally acceptable in schools. Undergirded by the NEA Code of Ethics, he analyzes some teacher behaviors that are generally unacceptable in most school districts.

Foreword

Dr. Osunde has approached student teaching from three perspectives: the students themselves, the new approaches for preparing teachers, and the theoretical underpinnings of the profession. His book should be very helpful for those committed to enhancing our nation's teacher education program.

Jessica S. Kozloff
President
Bloomsburg University of Pennsylvania

Acknowledgments

A scholarly work of this magnitude cannot be accomplished without contributions from many people. First, I want to recognize my mentors at the Ohio State University who have made significant impact on my life through the knowledge and skills I acquired from their classes and which I have in turn shared with my students for almost two decades. Prominent among these eminent educators are Professors Elsie Alberty, E. Ojo Arewa, Donald Cruickshank, Frederick Cyphert, Jack Frymier, M. Eugene Gilliom, Gail McCutcheon, Merry Merryfield, Anne Pruitt, Robert Silverman, and Robert Sutton.

Secondly, I want to acknowledge the student teachers with whom I have worked over the years. In particular, I appreciate and acknowledge the contributions of my former students and student teachers at Bloomsburg University of Pennsylvania: Diann M. Aikey, Jody L. Caboot, Christy Gengler, Brent J. Kelchner, Gregory Kellenberger, Tami J. Klinger, Mark E. Meloy, Meghan O'Donnell, Sonya Quick, Charles Taronis, and Christopher Yocum, for supplying materials and for their willingness to share their student teaching experiences. My thanks go to Christy Gengler and Dan Notari for their word-processing assistance. Thanks also to. Mary Osirim, Bryn Mawr College, Philadelphia, and Dr. Mary Alice Wheeler, Bloomsburg University of Pennsylvania, for reading and commenting on the first draft of this book's manuscript.

I would like to thank Dr. Ann L. Lee, Dean, College of Professional Studies, Bloomsburg University of Pennsylvania, for her support of my academic endeavors. Also, I am grateful to my colleagues, who have been extremely encouraging: Dr. Chris Cherrington; Dr. Hussein Fereshteh; Dr. Robert Gates, Assistant Dean, School of Education, and Director of Student Teaching Placement; Dr. Nancy Gilgannon; Dr. John Hranitz, Chairperson, Department of Curriculum and Foundations; Dr. Frank Keating; Dr. Frank Misiti; and others not listed here, in particular those who supervise student teachers, for their support and their useful ideas.

I must also acknowledge some wonderful school principals: Francis Libonati, Principal, Hazleton High School; Walter Lutz, Principal,

Acknowledgments

Berwick Middle School; Ned Sodrick, Principal, Shamokin Elementary School; and Richard Walton, Principal, Berwick High School. Thanks also to many helpful teachers, especially Thomas Gulash, Michelle Leitner, Bruce Lieb, Dr. David Sosar, and Robert Stevens, Hazleton High School; Mark Jarolen, Crestwood High School; Roslalee Aten, Robert Bower, Robert Buckley, Mary Jo Gibson, Beth Montana, and Robert Yeager, Berwick Area School District; Mary Zaikowski, Salem Elementary School; Francis Vottero, Shamokin High School; Jon Vastine, Southern Columbia High School; Jim Prosseda, Bloomsburg High School, and Susan Crisman, Central Columbia Middle School. These faculty members helped make my recent work with student teachers fun and successful.

Finally, I would like to thank some close friends and colleagues who have provided moral support and advice during difficult moments to further enhance my experiences at Bloomsburg University. These individuals include Dr. George Akeya Agbango, Maggie Boykin, Dr. Neil Brown, Kambon Camara, Dr. David Washburn, and Dr. Pamela Wynn. Other intimate friends and relations that I must acknowledge are the Reverend Fatoma Kpakiwa and Dr. Joseph Obi, Jr., of the University of Richmond; Dr. Jonathan Nwaobasi and Professor F. Odun Balogun of Delaware State University; Dr. Broderick Eribo, Howard University; Kester Abiodun Eke, Isaac Erhunmwensee, and Kingsley Ogbebor; and Andrew Ekue of the New York Public Schools. Also, I wish to express appreciation to my family members for their understanding during the long hours I have worked to complete this book.

Most of all, I want to thank the editors and staff of the University Press of America for their assistance in getting this work published. In particular, I want to mention Peter Cooper, Helen Hudson, and Nancy J. Ulrich, the immediate past acquisition editor of UPA. Also, I want to thank Jane Rea, EEI Communications, Dorothy Albritton, Majestic Wordsmith, and Carol Claudon, for their contributions in the production of this book. Finally, I am grateful to Phi Delta Kappa, the National Education Association, Dr. Alex J. Dubil, Superintendent, Bloomsburg Area School District, and the Ohio State University, College of Education's Global Education Program, for their permission to use materials from their publications in this book.

Egerton O. Osunde, Ph.D.
Bloomsburg University of Pennsylvania

Introduction

For most students in teacher education programs, student teaching remains the most challenging aspect of their studies. Despite taking several courses about the theory and practice of teaching and accumulating many classroom observation hours, many students remain unsure of what to expect while student teaching. At first, student teachers are nervous and often intimidated by the restlessness of students. They are confused about how to adopt an appropriate classroom control and discipline policy. Amazed by the amount of work involved with lesson preparation, student teachers often become angry about sacrificing personal relaxation time. Many are upset by the inferior treatment they receive from full-time teachers and staff, who may not fully accept student teachers as colleagues. At the same time, they are bewildered by school policies and rules. These experiences can be traumatizing for many college students. In fact, the emotional effects can be so devastating that some students withdraw from student teaching. Thus, there is a need to help students become aware of what is expected of them during their student teaching experiences. It seems that current teacher education programs do not provide students with adequate insight into the nature of student teaching.

Reading about the student teaching experiences of others is an excellent way for students to learn how to deal with the challenges presented by student teaching. It allows them to vicariously place themselves in various teaching positions. I have used this technique in my student teaching seminars and have found it to be quite effective.Many of my students have said how useful it was to learn from other student teachers or the experiences of first-year teachers. Thus, much of what I have revealed in this book is information shared by my students during student teaching seminars, written by them in daily journals, or expressed to me during personal conversations. In addition, I have included ideas expressed by cooperating teachers in workshops we organized in recent years at Bloomsburg University focusing on student teaching supervision.

This book's opening chapter addresses an issue of principal concern to student teachers: the fears of being a student teacher. The second chapter analyzes supervisors' and cooperating teachers' expectations of student teachers. The third chapter presents seven cases designed to help student teachers form adequate expectations and consider the best approaches to different classroom situations. The cases presented in this book cover the experiences of student teachers and a first-year teacher, to provide a contrast between student teaching and teaching as a career. The cases detail actual experiences of a selected number of student teachers I have supervised over the years. These teachers have agreed to contribute to the improvement of student teaching by sharing their experiences with others. The cases describe experiences of both elementary and secondary school student teachers, covering student and student teacher interaction, classroom control and discipline, instructional strategies, quality of learning activities, school policies and rules, and other specific challenges. For confidentiality, the names of cooperating teachers have been omitted, and the names of the cooperating schools were changed. The fourth chapter offers strategies for dealing with some of the common student teaching problems mentioned in the cases in chapter 3, including classroom management and discipline. Chapter 5 deals with teaching in a block or intensive scheduled school. Chapter 6 focuses on teacher instructional behavior in an inclusive and culturally diverse classroom. Chapters 7 concern evaluations in student teaching. In chapter 8, several sample evaluation forms are presented to provide student teachers with a clear understanding of the criteria used to assess student teaching. In chapter 9, student teachers' attention is drawn to a matter often taken for granted: the code of ethics for teachers. The book concludes with a glossary that presents definitions of commonly used concepts in teacher education.

Chapter 1

ℰℭ

Fears of Being a Student Teacher

S tudents often look forward to student teaching. Unfortunately, this excitement is replaced by anxiety and nervousness the moment students see the student teaching placement schedule or show up for their first day at their new school. It is natural for students to experience fears and uncertainty as they go into student teaching. Typical student teachers' fears include how they will be accepted by the students, the cooperating teacher, and other staff in the building; whether they have adequate knowledge of the subject matter and pedagogy; whether they will be able to plan for actual instruction; whether they will be able to teach in the presence of the cooperating teacher and college supervisor; whether they will be able to establish themselves as a teacher; and whether they will be able to manage the classroom.

Student teachers are always concerned about how they will be received by their cooperating teachers and students. They can also be anxious about how to develop high-quality relationships with the other teachers, school principal, vice principal, librarian, office staff, and other workers in the building. Many of these fears can be alleviated if the student teacher places a phone call to the cooperating teacher and arranges to visit (preferably, for a full day) one or two weeks prior to the beginning of student teaching. During this visit, the student teacher will be able to meet with the cooperating teacher and interact with the students. The cooperating teacher and student teacher can discuss teaching philosophy, classroom management styles, and the school curriculum. A tour of the school with the cooperating teacher and an introduction of the student teacher to other staff members in the building would also help the student teacher feel welcome and have less anxiety when student teaching begins.

Another area of concern for student teachers is learning the names of students in their classroom. Student teachers in elementary schools may find it fairly easy to learn the names of the 25 to 30 students in their classes. In contrast, student teachers in high schools may have trouble learning the names of the 30 to 100 students who rotate in and out of their classrooms. It is advisable that student teachers develop a seating chart for each class on the first day and try to memorize every name. Calling students by their names during instruction can help student teachers learn names more quickly.

Student teachers may also be anxious about whether they have adequate knowledge of the subject matter. There is the fear that they will be tested by the students, cooperating teacher, and college supervisor. It is important to realize that these fears are normal. Student teachers have to understand that student teaching is a learning experience and that they are not expected to have complete mastery of subject matter or be able to perform like a "master teacher." Most college supervisors and cooperating teachers are understanding about occasional mistakes. Student teachers should be willing to accept that they made a mistake and that they do not have answers to all questions posed by the students. In case of a difficult question, student teachers should explain that they do not have an answer but would be happy to seek one out..

Closely related to this anxiety about knowledge is the anxiety over instructional strategies. Student teachers are concerned about whether cooperating teachers will give them freedom to implement previously learned teaching strategies, educational philosophies, and evaluation and measurement practices. While some cooperating teachers grant ample freedom, some others do not, and student teachers fear they will be directed to solely imitate the mannerisms, teaching style, and classroom management policies of their cooperating teacher. Student teachers also wonder if their instructional content is appropriate for student ability levels and if their tests will genuinely measure student ability and reflect the material that has been covered.

Student teachers often experience anxiety related to classroom management and discipline. They wonder whether they should adopt the cooperating teacher's classroom discipline and management style or introduce something different. Student teachers, because of a lack of experience, are often unsure about their leadership and classroom control abilities. They wonder if they have the strength to be firm, fair, and consistent. Moreover, there is concern about how to establish themselves as teachers. At the kindergarten and lower grades of the elementary level, the students are often used to interacting with parent volunteers and student observers, but they are not used to another teacher taking over instruction while their primary teacher sits behind them or leaves the classroom. The students have difficulty trusting another teacher. As a result, the students generally prefer to go to the cooperating teacher when they have questions or need help. When cooperating teachers leave the classroom, the students are likely to ask student teachers where the cooperating teachers went or when they will be back. Cooperating teachers should help student teachers establish themselves as teachers by redirecting the children to speak with or obtain help from student teachers. The students should be encouraged to perceive the student teacher as someone who can be trusted and who is in control.

Furthermore, many student teachers fear that they will not be able to adequately deal with the complex issues involved with inclusion. Since enactment of the federal act Public Law 94-142, the Education for All Handicapped Children Act, mixed-ability classrooms have become the norm, and every teacher must expect to have one. In a mixed-ability classroom, student teachers should design lessons so that most students will understand. The lessons should also allow for independent practice so that, if necessary, students can work independently at their own pace. In this instance, it is the student teachers' responsibility to ensure that each child keep up with and finish each assignment. Furthermore, student teachers must evaluate each student's work according to his or her individual ability. Meanwhile, most school districts provide additional assistance—by employing teacher aids who work with severely handicapped children, for instance.

Student teachers' fears dissipate as they teach more and more classes and as they begin to have a better understanding of their students, teaching styles, goals, and educational philosophy. In addition, student teachers gain self-confidence once they have established open communication with their cooperating teacher and other faculty members, and once they begin to feel comfortable in their new teaching role. In conclusion, it should be reiterated that student teachers' fears, and the nervousness that accompanies them, are perfectly normal. Student teachers should feel free to voice these fears and seek reassurance from friends, cooperating teachers, and student teaching supervisors.

Chapter 2

ഇൻരു

Supervisor and Cooperating Teacher Expectations

W hat are the expectations of cooperating teachers for student teachers? This question has been the focus of discussion in workshops that we have organized at Bloomsburg University for both experienced and newly appointed cooperating teachers. The relevance of this question cannot be overemphasized. Student teachers are expected to demonstrate certain abilities and qualities associated with their training and the field of teaching as a whole. Knowing the expectations of cooperating teachers and student teaching supervisors can relieve much anxiety, because knowing what is expected is the key to success. It is difficult, if not impossible, for student teachers to perform well if they do not know how their performance is being evaluated.

Our analysis of responses gathered from the workshops shows that cooperating teachers and student teaching supervisors expect student teachers to demonstrate a positive attitude, a willingness to learn, and a desire for professional growth. Student teachers must show that they are genuinely interested in teaching. They must demonstrate enthusiasm and initiative, the ability to make decisions and take action without instruction from the cooperating teacher. The ability to "jump in" can significantly improve how cooperating teachers and school administrators think of student teachers. Cooperating teachers and supervisors also expect student teachers to demonstrate subject matter competency. Student teachers should be able to show mastery of subject matter and adequate knowledge of the research materials in their discipline. Student teachers should be willing to search for additional materials from outside sources to supplement the classroom textbook. Cooperating teachers and supervisors do not expect student teachers to be able to handle all situations perfectly. After all, student teaching is truly a learning experience. However, it is expected that student teachers will approach their duties with enthusiasm, dedication, and professionalism.

Student teachers need to demonstrate their knowledge by applying theory to practice. They should be able to use personal experiences to illustrate theoretical concepts. Students are easily motivated if teachers can explain abstract concepts using events occurring in students' immediate environment. Moreover, student teachers must assume the full responsibilities of a teacher and be willing to work with other adults or instructional aids in the classroom. Student teachers must demonstrate to the students that they are in full control by making important decisions in the classroom. Student teachers should not encourage students to go to the cooperating teacher (who may be sitting somewhere at the back of the classroom) for permission to use the bathroom, leave the classroom to run minor errands, or accomplish similar tasks. It is not expected, and in many cases is undesirable, for a student teacher to be loved by all students. Nevertheless, student teachers must be accepting, empathetic, and professional and provide structure to all of their students.

Possessing a willingness to learn and a desire for professional growth is essential if student teachers are to fully benefit from their field experiences. More specifically, student teachers must take risks, contributing to and adapting to new teaching experiences. To achieve professional growth, student teachers must also be able to ask for, accept, and learn from constructive criticism.

Establishing a positive professional relationship with a cooperating teacher is essential. The cooperating teacher possesses wisdom that can enhance the student teaching experience. Although student teachers are encouraged to try to implement their own teaching strategies and not to copy the cooperating teacher wholly, they must be willing to learn by example, sometimes modeling their cooperating teachers (Osunde, 1996). Student teachers need to be able to identify and act on cues from their cooperating teachers, and they should feel comfortable asking questions and accepting con-structive criticism. Honest communication will reduce anxiety, make student teaching easier, and help student teachers reach their full potential in the profession.

College Supervisor observes student teacher instructional interaction with students. Courtesy: Berwick Area Middle School.

Chapter 3

၆ာ

Accounts of Student Teaching Experiences

The following case studies present analyses of student teaching experiences. The stories differ from individual to individual and from institution to institution. To a great extent, the differences can be attributed to the teaching context, the personalities of the student teachers, and the student teachers' interaction with students and faculty. Many problems identified by the student teachers in these case studies will be carefully analyzed in chapter 4.

Cooperative learning group. Courtesy: Central Columbia Middle School

Case Study 1:

My Experiences as a Student Teacher in Utopian Area High School and Junior High School

Christy Marie

Case Study 1

Throughout my first and second placements as a student teacher in the Utopian Area School District, I encountered several problems that I had not anticipated. My expectations about possible difficulties were often inaccurate; what I assumed would be difficult was often the easiest part of the job. Furthermore, what was easy in one student placement was sometimes difficult in the next. Like many student teachers, I found that almost nothing remained consistent from one placement to the next.

I assumed that the most difficult task of my first placement would be controlling classes and establishing myself as a teacher. This was not the case. My cooperating teacher eased me into the teaching role. I began by taking over the homeroom, progressed to teaching one class for a week, and assumed responsibilities for all classes the following week. My cooperating teacher supported my position as the new classroom authority by answering all student requests with the comment "Go ask your teacher." This approach, combined with his frequent absence from the classroom, allowed me to rapidly establish my authority as a teacher. After I learned to be comfortable with denying unreasonable student requests, my authority was in place. A good rapport with students followed. I attribute this to learning student names rapidly and showing students respect.

My classes, Sociology and Psychology, were electives for juniors and seniors. Because students willingly selected these classes, I found that most students wanted to be in class and were eager to learn about the subject matter. However, there were two other results of the elective course status that I did not anticipate. First, the heterogeneous nature of the classes led to several difficulties with pacing the material that I taught. Second, the students expected the course to be easier than required courses.

Pacing and trying to plan activities for an allotted time period was by far the most difficult part of beginning my placement. I was horrified by the uncertainty of the time needed to complete activities, and for my first two days of teaching, classroom activities ran counter to expected time frames. To add to the uncertainty, lessons took a varied amount of time from class to class because of interruptions and differences in how quickly material could be presented. I found it helpful to break activities down into 15-minute intervals and to have an extra activity planned in case of additional time or unanticipated events.

Another pacing problem that I encountered concerned individual student needs. The heterogeneous nature of the group led to a class of varied academic ability. A review that might seem redundant to some students was greatly desired by others. A few students expressed boredom when material was reinforced. I had no idea that individual needs would necessitate planning for student groups as well as for the class as a whole. My main goal was to ensure broad student understanding of presented material. Yet I did not want to alienate the accelerated students with repetition. Extra credit and optional assignments seemed to fill the time gap created when some students needed more review than others.

Because of the elective course status, many students expected an easy A or B and seemed surprised by my high expectations for their performance. My expectations rarely matched student performance. A few students did consistently well, but for the most part, I encountered poor spelling and grammar, incomplete homework assignments, students unprepared for tests, and, as a result, low test grades. After grading my first test, I questioned my abilities as a teacher. Had I tested what was taught? Was the test too difficult? Were my expectations extremely high? I took several steps to set my mind at ease. I read appropriate essay question responses to the class to clearly convey my expectations and told them that sentence and paragraph form were required. I asked students who failed if they had studied. Ninety-nine percent admitted they had not. Prior to testing, I composed two or three test questions immediately after presenting the material, therefore ensuring that my objectives and test questions corresponded. I also presented my ungratified expectation problem to colleagues.

'My colleagues responded by discussing this paradox: How do you distinguish teacher and student responsibility for grading purposes? Our discussion focused on failing students. We decided that teacher responsibilities included motivating students, conveying lessons with clarity, and providing additional help for students who encounter difficulties. Student responsibilities included being attentive and studying. Yet I still felt that I had failed when a student received a poor grade, even if he or she had not studied. I obviously had not motivated these students to achieve. The teachers and I concluded that the only way to feel good about my job performance was to assure myself that I had truly given my best effort.

My most frequent classroom management problems were off-task students talking among themselves, cheating, and the confusion created by unanticipated yet routine classroom disruptions. To combat most off-task behavior, I used body language. Looking directly at someone usually did the trick. If it did not, I often asked if I was interrupting a student conversation. I did not hesitate to move students. After only a few days of teaching, I could identify possible problem areas and adjust seating as necessary. I encountered several problems with students copying homework from one another. This was particularly obvious when word-for-word replicas appeared during opinion assignments. To prevent cheating, I made a general classroom announcement that work should be completed individually unless I instructed them otherwise. I acted as if I were doing the guilty parties a favor. Seeing little benefit to failing students for copying, I offered an option: They could take the failing grade, or they could redo the assignment for the next day and it would be graded as a day late.

A personal difficulty that arose during my first placement was adjusting to the hours of the job. Writing goals and objectives, grading papers, planning activities for classes, sequencing units and topics, creating tests, studying subject matter, and constantly evaluating my performance were extremely time-consuming. An hour commute made my day even longer. There were some mornings when I would wake up and say aloud, "I don't want to be a teacher." Once I adjusted to a teacher's schedule, my negative attitude toward teaching faded. With my second placement, the subject matter was less complex, and I had to plan for only one course. Free time began to trickle back into my life.

My second placement presented different challenges. My new cooperating teacher had never had a student teacher before. Therefore, he was hesitant to leave the room, cautious about which activities his classes could handle, and concerned about student behavior. It disturbed me that my cooperating teacher did not leave me alone with his classes. He spent most of his time in a partitioned office in the classroom. This allowed him to hear but not see classroom activities. He rarely interjected, but occasionally he felt a need to discipline students. When I thought I had ingeniously solved a problem or dealt with a situation appropriately, he would sometimes attempt to handle the situation himself after class. This placed me in an awkward position and undermined the authority I had tried to achieve.

My cooperating teacher's ideas about classroom management differed greatly from my own. To direct student attention and behavior, he most often raised his voice. I tried to choose more subtle ways of dealing with undesirable behavior and concentrate as much as possible on prevention. As I began to realize, my co-op felt a need to discipline because he thought I was not disciplining at all. He could not hear the quiet chats that accompanied behavior problems when I was in charge. To make matters worse, I was afraid of offending my co-op or making myself look weak by presenting our differences in disciplinary approaches. After presenting my opinions to my co-op, his interjections became less frequent, but our differences in disciplinary styles remained present during the entire placement.

My experience teaching the seventh grade led me to discover the problems associated with labeling and the difficulty of grading different ability groups for the same class content. Homogeneous grouping created a situation in which classes seemed to be divided into three labeled categories. The accelerated students were labeled "bright," "grade conscious," and "good workers" and generally were compliant in the classroom. The support-group classes seemed to be composed of second- or third-time repeat seventh graders, students with behavior problems, and below-level achievers commonly viewed as "lazy." The last category was that of average seventh graders. These students were labeled as very "compliant" in the classroom; however, teachers viewed them as students who would do little beyond the minimum requirements to achieve a grade.

I was exposed to very little individual labeling in my first placement because of the heterogeneous nature of the classes. I found the labels at the seventh-grade level disconcerting; it seemed that the labels might prevent some students from achieving their full potential. I could only speculate about how labeling might influence classroom performance. Although I planned on giving adapted tests for each ability level, I approached these labels skeptically and held consistently high expectations for all classes.

Homogeneous grouping also presented an unsettling grading paradox. Support-group students took adapted and slightly easier tests, while accelerated classes took more difficult tests. If a support-group student scored a B on a test, and an accelerated student received a C on a more difficult test, how could I accurately assign grades? Clearly, averaging test scores would paint an inaccurate picture of academic achievement. Therefore, I averaged class participation, homework, and creative projects with test scores to create a more adequate grading policy. Ironically, the students who needed the grade boost offered by these projects rarely completed them.

As with my previous placement, my expectations rarely matched overall student performance. Many students made no attempt to answer essay questions. Some skipped completion questions even though I provided possible answers for the section. On the other hand, some seventh-grade essays were of higher quality than essays that I had encountered at the high school level.

Pacing problems with my diverse seventh-grade students were similar to grading problems but even more complex. A "hidden curriculum" added to lesson completion time. Students were learning and practicing note taking, outlining, summarizing, map reading, and interpreting charts and graphs. Many students needed practice with reading. Reviews for tests were much more comprehensive than at the high school level. Student confusion often warranted a slow pace, frequent reinforcement of learning, and sometimes reteaching of lessons. Classroom distractions often made it impossible to gauge the time required for a lesson.

Distractions included physical and mental disruptions of learning. Announcements from the principal and student requests, in addition to late arrivals and early dismissals, were among the physical distractions. It always amazed me how easy it was to influence student behavior. The presence of others in the room, the time of day, the day of the week, and the weather all seemed to cause changes in student behavior. It was difficult to focus the attention of a seventh grader.

Behavior was also influenced by the class chemistry. The combinations of personalities in each class provided many truly unique teaching experiences. If a few students were absent, a normally outgoing and frequently off-topic class might become shy and work extremely well throughout the entire period. Some classes just seemed to be moody: up one day and down the next. Without my ever being able to accurately predict student behavior, adaptations to instruction were always necessary.

Other than individual student problems, classroom management problems were minimized by a set of procedures reviewed frequently by each class. Common class management problems included note passing and off-task talking among students. Both of these were, for the most part, solved by seating chart adjustments. Student disruptions were most frequently caused by limited attention spans and high levels of energy. This brought me to another challenge: How do you correct the behavior of a student who is not intentionally disruptive but disruptive all the same? When I asked colleagues for help with this situation, I received a wide variety of conflicting solutions ranging in scale from detention to ignoring the behavior. It required a great deal of patience to gauge my expectations for the seventh-grade level. I tried to incorporate stray comments and actions into the lesson, and I corrected frequent offenders with reminders.

A specific problem that I encountered involved Mike, a student who periodically refused to complete class activities and even tests. One day, after expressing discontent about taking a test, Mike scribbled squiggly lines on his answer sheet and completed the test within 30 seconds. I collected his test without interrupting the class and decided to address the issue later. After I was fully briefed on Mike's home life, the reasons for his behavior problems became apparent. Mike was largely abandoned as a small child and had little, if any, positive family influence. Mike quickly conveyed to me that he did not care about school and used his home life, or lack thereof, as an excuse not to try.

With this in mind, I took the test to the vice principal and explained the situation. He contacted the staff members at Mike's residence and sent them a copy of the test. The staff agreed to work with Mike on this matter, and a week later the staff initiated teacher conferences to maintain awareness of Mike's assignments and his progress. We discussed behavior problems and special needs at these meetings. I was thrilled with this development. I was glad to have played a small part in improving Mike's situation.

At the completion of my student teaching experiences, I assessed my progress. My instructional behavior had become much more flexible, and I had successfully implemented many procedures and fulfilled most of my expectations with each class. I had experimented with various teaching techniques and varied sequencing of lessons from class to class. However, many teaching difficulties eluded a perfect solution, and I still felt like a failure when students did poorly on evaluations.

Although I taught in the same school district for both placements, each placement was a unique experience that offered different problems and demanded different solutions. My high school experience only slightly prepared me for the junior high world, but it gave me the confidence and insight to adapt well. In the end, my prior expectations about student teaching were disproved by both placements.

Case Study 2:

My Experiences as a Student Teacher in Smithfield Area Middle School and Berry High School and as a First-Year Teacher in the Vistas County Public School System

Mark

Case Study 2

D espite what you may hear in the time leading up to your field experience, nothing truly prepares you for student teaching. The same may be said for the first day of your professional career. You can read and examine documents dealing with hypothetical classroom situations, but the key element that is missing is people. Individuals have different personalities, different viewpoints, and yes, different ways of dealing with situations that may arise in the classroom. While reading about and imagining possible classroom scenarios is helpful and necessary, the only real way to prepare is to practice. Practice requires you to react, and training helps you know your options. Without adequate reactions, situations can quickly deteriorate. I hope that some of the information I share will help you to prepare for student teaching. At the same time, I hope I may alleviate some of your anxiety.

My initial advice is this: Be totally serious about your student teaching and do not view it as something that you want to pass through quickly and painlessly. View it instead as a chance to practice what you have learned, try some new things, and work in a situation that will help you feel confident as you take risks. Take advantage of the opportunity to work without fear of failure.

Student teaching is a safety net that helps you train for your profession, not a final evaluation of your aptitude as a teacher. If you have initial anxiety, it is a good sign. If you are not worried at all, you may be seen as not taking your situation seriously. No matter how nervous you are, remember that you are supposed to have successes and failures, good and bad days, and problems. How you deal with these problems is important. Will you say, "This lesson was a joke today, but if I adapt the activity so that all can participate, it may run more smoothly," or will you see it as a catastrophe that may never be repaired?

Having made it through my first professional year with the Vistas County Public School System, I have the unique opportunity to share experiences from both my current position and my student teaching. I am sure you may have heard much of what I will tell you, but that is why I consider it sound advice. Let me start by saying that you are fortunate to have a 16-week student teaching experience. I have spoken with many teachers who had just 8 weeks of field experience. Many of these people wished that they had done more or that they had covered a situation that came up very early in their first year of teaching. Nothing can fully prepare you for the first year of teaching, but 16 weeks are better than 8.

My first student teaching assignment was at Smithfield Area Middle School. I had the good fortune of being placed with a well-respected member of the faculty who had more than 20 years of teaching experience. He combined his experience with real energy and a willingness to create fun and motivating activities for his students. I was very nervous, yet very grateful. I would be able to rely on his great experience, yet at the same time, I would have to work hard to keep up with his pace. My anxiety was probably unnecessary, for a student teacher is not expected to act or perform exactly like a teacher with over 20 years of experience. Remember that you are there to learn! Do not put undue stress on yourself by trying to hit a home run every day.

It is very important that you be the one to initiate a dialogue with your cooperative teacher. Your co-op has managed a routine for years and may not want to feel as if he or she is pressuring you by always initiating conversation. If you know your assignment early enough, you should send an introductory letter to your co-op. I sent a letter to each of my cooperating teachers and was able to schedule observations prior to the start of my student teaching assignments. By doing this, I resolved several questions and alleviated much of that first-day anxiety.

The first week of your assignment is important, for you will probably be observing. Use this time to study your co-op's strategies and classroom management techniques. Don't be afraid to ask questions. Ask your co-op how he or she has dealt with certain actual or hypothetical situations. During the observation period, you may see a strategy or activity that you want to try later. This is your chance to familiarize yourself with the school, classroom, and most important, the library and resource room. Finding resources during the first week may reduce the amount of time you spend searching and scrambling later in your experience.

Once you have a class or two, you will begin to get a feel for what you need to do. Once I took over all the classes, I knew the names of all the students. This is a necessity! Students want you to know their names, just as you want them to address you appropriately.

Lesson plan strategies are nice, and motivating activities are great, but how you teach is most dependent on how effectively you manage your class. Do not try to be friends with the students. Students, especially high school students, may try to become friends with you because of your closeness in age. Be professional. You are there to do a job, and while it is important to build a rapport with your students, a meaningful rapport takes time. Students may try to earn a quick "friendship" and call on it when they need it. Allow friendships to come, but don't actively seek them.

Consult your co-op to clarify his or her classroom rules and expectations. Use the rules that are already in place. Be firm and consistent. This is the key. There is no need to be overly aggressive, but it is essential to be firm and consistent. For example, if you tell a student that a repeated behavior will result in detention or some other consequence, then you must implement the punishment if that repeated behavior occurs. If you do not, you will have shown the students that they can do anything because they know that you will not deliver a promised punishment. Do not be afraid to lay ground rules and to stick to them. If you are consistent in your classroom management practices, you will have control of the class, which is absolutely necessary if you want to try new and exciting interactive activities.

Class size is a key factor in classroom management. In both my assignments, the classes were small. At Smithfield, my largest class consisted of 21 students. At my second assignment, Berry High School, my largest class had 24 students. A smaller class size made classroom management easier. There were fewer people to watch, I knew more about each individual, and student-involved activities could be organized and started quickly. At Vistas High School, my smallest class had 21 students, and two of the five classes were larger than 25 students. This made classroom management strategies a priority as I began the year. Make classroom management your priority too.

In one aspect, student teaching may have been more difficult than my first year of teaching: The subjects I taught were more numerous during student teaching. For example, at Berry High School, my cooperative teacher allowed me to teach all of the classes, after an appropriate period of time. My co-op had 20 years of teaching experience and a background in economics that allowed him to teach an elective economics course for gifted seniors. After two weeks in Berry, I was preparing each night for tenth-grade Pennsylvania Civics, two sections of ninth-grade U.S. History, eleventh-grade Government, and the twelfth-grade economics course. This was a real challenge, and I was very busy. At Vistas, I had a schedule of five classes: three sections of ninth-grade World History and two sections of tenth-grade World Studies II. This meant that I needed to prepare for only two different classes, although classes' different skill levels and learning styles demanded alterations in lesson activities. It is unlikely that you will have five different classes to prepare for during student teaching, but three would give you a good idea of the amount of preparation time involved in a normal teaching schedule.

The student bodies at the schools where I have taught have been very different. At Smithfield and Berry, the classes were fairly homogeneous. Students were predominantly white middle-class boys and girls who spoke English. At Vistas, however, there were students of many races and ethnic groups. For example, most of my classes consisted of over 50 percent non-Hispanic white students. Of these, almost all spoke fluent English. The remaining 40 to 50 percent were mostly Hispanic students and smaller numbers of African Americans, Korean Americans, Vietnamese Americans, and other groups from the Far East. Many of these students spoke English at varying levels of ability. During student teaching, I questioned the value of studying multiculturalism and cultural diversity. Well, now I know. Unless you are placed in an urban environment for your student teaching experience, you may not need all of the multicultural training. But it is very necessary. The nation is increasingly diverse, and I am using multicultural strategies daily.

I have already mentioned that it is good to have a short but concise set of ground rules in place when you enter the classroom, but it is just as important to be flexible. Kids like firmness and fairness. Some of the best classroom management situations at Vistas occurred when a student had tested the bounds of acceptable classroom behavior and had to face the consequences. By applying appropriate punishment to the infraction (punishment students were aware of well in advance), I let students know that the class came first and order would prevail.

What adds to classroom management is something that doesn't necessarily take place in class: building a strong line of communication between the teacher and parents. Nine times out of ten, such communication results in excellent reinforcement for the student, and if done early enough, it places you and the parents in a zone of understanding. I have had great successes with phone calls this year. For example, in the middle of the third quarter, student X's grades began to falter and her behavior began to decline as well. I immediately called home without telling the student beforehand. I explained to the mother that I was calling because I had been pleased with X's progress earlier, but I was starting to become concerned, and I then told the mother the basis for my concern. I spent a few minutes answering the mother's questions and suggesting methods to help. The next day X's behavior adjusted, and soon after that her grades rose again. That call was important in two ways. First, the parents were aware that I was concerned, not angry, and they were given the facts of the situation. Also, the student saw that my rules and expectations could not be ignored. In this example, it helped that the parents were playing a strong role in their child's life, which may not always be the case. Communication ultimately helped the classroom management situation.

I recommend that you try this approach (if necessary) even while student teaching. Poor grades and disciplinary infractions are not the only situations that warrant parent calls. I made many phone calls to express how happy I was with a student's progress. The parents love it, because teacher–parent conversations usually involve bad news. No matter what the next phone call may hold, the parents will be in your corner. The kids, after receiving parental praise, often strive to improve their performance because they enjoyed positive reinforcement. In Vistas County, teachers are encouraged to maintain records of all home calls, and I would encourage you to do the same.

You are probably asking yourself, "What am I going to do once I am in the classroom?" I do not have any specific strategies or activities for you, but I can tell you how to avoid unnecessary hours of work and a few headaches. First, it is not always necessary to "reinvent the wheel." Every lesson does not have to be totally new. Ask your colleagues what has worked best for them. Most teachers are happy to share ideas and are equally happy to receive new ideas.

I can best describe what to expect in the classroom by discussing lesson plans. You should establish two or three measurable objectives for each class period. In a 50-minute class period, you should be able to successfully cover two to three objectives, but this is a flexible number. Objectives should be meaningful and to the point.

Your lesson should have a clear topic, and a brief daily content outline may follow the objectives. The objectives and the content outline can be placed on the chalkboard to give the students a focus. You will also find that the content outline can serve as an itinerary for your class, and this itinerary may help you make transitions in your lesson. Next, some type of initiation activity will motivate and further focus the students. I have often used a classwide discussion question to stimulate thoughts about upcoming material. Simulations and small-group activities may also serve as initiation activities.

The largest portion of your lesson will involve teaching strategies, or different means of transmitting content. Any activity that lasts longer than 15 minutes may cause problems because of limited student attention spans. Try to use a variety of strategies—perhaps an interactive bulletin board activity or a visual presentation that requires students to contribute deleted bits of information. Basically, lesson strategies consist of individual or group activities, puzzles, projects, and student presentations. I usually lecture in only five- to ten-minute intervals. There is room for lectures in high school, but use them sparingly. If you lecture for 30 or 40 minutes, you'll be dead! Using an overhead transparency presentation in conjunction with lecture information helps to draw students into a lesson.

In your lesson plan, you should also explain how you intend to measure student learning. You should have some activity that will serve as an evaluation, whether it be an oral or written quiz or an individual writing exercise. There are many evaluation tools, and it is imperative to include some form of measurement in each lesson. Your written lesson plan should finish with a list of materials that you will need for the lesson and a bibliography of materials used to support the lesson.

The end of your actual classroom lesson should have some type of closure. Examples of closure range from student summaries of the day's lesson to instructor explanations about the relationship between the lesson and the unit theme. Daily closure will provide continuity to your classes.

The last items I would like to share are what I consider my most trusted "survival tips." First, be prepared to be overwhelmed. As I mentioned earlier, nothing will truly prepare you for your first professional year of teaching. You will come across loads of information, ranging from school policies to various types of individual student data. Do not feel that you must absorb it all overnight, or you'll quickly become stressed. Peruse the information in pieces, and it will be easier.

Second, be organized and prepared. In fact, always be overprepared for class. It is better to have to move items from one day's lesson to the next day's lesson than to teach for 20 minutes and allow the students to spend the remaining 30 minutes inventing ways to entertain themselves. Preparation prevents unnecessary classroom management problems.

Next, do not become isolated. With so much to do there will be a tendency to lock yourself in a room with piles of papers and become a hermit. Talk to other teachers and share your ideas and questions. This will help you make connections and help you in your planning. I plan with two other World Studies teachers, and we all have benefited from the exchange of ideas. Remember, two or more heads are better than one. It is also important to be a good listener. Don't be drawn into becoming a school "activist." As the new kid on the block, you should want to listen and learn. Better things will come to a humble and conscientious listener.

Next, try to involve yourself in activities outside the classroom. This helps you establish a good rapport with students, and it shows them that you are accessible. Some of my best experiences have been monitoring the weight room and helping to build the freshman class float for the homecoming parade.

Finally, understand that teaching is a serious full-time job. You will be working more than 40 hours a week and planning on weekends. Some days you will have to work at school until 5:00 or 6:00 P.M. You may need to visit the school on the weekends to use the photocopier and plan. Use part of the summer for a break and spend the remainder of it planning for the next year or taking courses for your professional development. I am currently taking a "Spanish for Educators" course to help me with many of the Hispanic students that will be in my classes this coming schoolyear.

There is so much more I want to share with you, but some things you will just have to experience on your own. This essay is not a "golden set of rules," and I do not know everything. I make plenty of mistakes, and I learn from them. I hope that some of this information has been helpful, and I wish you all the best in your student teaching and in your professional career to come.

Case Study 3:

My Experiences as a Student Teacher in Brookfield Area High School and Utopian Area High School

Diann

Case Study 3

My expectations prior to my actual student teaching experience were based on field study experiences and course work. Before student teaching, I spent 45 hours in the classroom during field studies, and I took several classes to help prepare me for student teaching. Neither the classes nor the field studies can fully prepare you for what you encounter during student teaching. I was unprepared for the amount of preparation, organization, and planning involved with student teaching. Nor did I anticipate how rewarding the experience would be.

My first student teaching experience was at Brookfield Area High School. For the first week, I observed my cooperating teacher and several other teachers, many of whom primarily used a lecture/discussion style of teaching. This worried me. I feared that the students wouldn't be receptive to some of the innovative methods that I learned in my college classes.

The students were very enthusiastic about my presence in the classroom. They asked many personal questions. I tried to be open with them, but this was a mistake. I was too friendly with the students. I should have answered their questions in a manner that would help reinforce a professional student–teacher relationship. It was difficult to maintain discipline and classroom control once I had become too friendly with the students.

My second mistake in maintaining classroom control was to use my co-op's disciplinary policy. My co-op's methods didn't work for me for several reasons. First, I was uncomfortable in a loosely disciplined atmosphere. I lacked my co-op's previously established respect. I stepped in as a new student teacher and expected to receive the same level of respect. This did not happen. Not only did I need to earn the respect of the students, I needed to demand it. Initially, I did not assert myself and demand classroom control, and for the rest of my time at Brookfield, I struggled with disciplinary problems.

I didn't have just one or two disciplinary problem students. I had nine students who continually tried to disrupt a general tenth-grade class on a daily basis. I was unable to regain control of this class for the entire placement. Yet I was able to regain control in other classes by using several methods.

To regain control, I used a class participation point system in which the students lost points for disruptive behavior. Class would stop until the disruptive behavior ceased. Another method I used was to stand directly beside the disruptive student. My presence alone often deterred the negative behavior. If none of these methods worked, I would say the student's name out loud and tell him or her to stop. In most cases, the embarrassment would curtail the behavior. As a last resort, I would pull the student aside, either before or after class, to discuss the problem. This was necessary only twice, and in both cases, the student was apologetic when not among his or her peers.

Despite these efforts, there continued to be disciplinary problems that might not have occurred if I had been more firm and confident from the beginning. But my self-confidence increased with better preparation, and student attentiveness increased with my self-confidence.

The experience was not all negative. There were several positive aspects that made me feel good about my teaching ability and methods. My older and more scholarly students enjoyed some of the strategies I used and showed much enthusiasm. For example, I initiated a current-events day each Friday in my twelfth-grade Problems of Democracy classes. The students loved debating and discussing current events in government. These days were also educational for me. I had no idea adolescents could be so conservative. Their conservative attitudes may have been influenced by the community and parents.

The students seemed to enjoy a variety of my planned activities. They developed a political platform for a simulated political party. The students also put forth a competitive effort. I was proud when my students showed such initiative. I created an Asian culture day lesson for my World Geography class. My students had several days to prepare. When the culture day arrived, the students had done such a thorough job, we could have spent three days sharing all they had discovered. As a student teacher, I received great satisfaction from motivating the students to do such a good job.

The aspect of my teaching experience at Brookfield Area High School that I was most proud of was my ability to get students to participate who, according to my co-op, had not previously participated at all. I called on students who hid, and by the end of my time there, I had many of these students actively raising their hands.

My second student teaching experience was at Utopian Area High School. I observed for several days before taking control of the class. Again, I observed several other teachers and noticed that they primarily used a lecture/discussion method. In this case, however, my future students asked me several times, "Are we going to do anything fun?" From the beginning, therefore, I was aware of their expectations.

My cooperating teacher had developed and maintained a very disciplined classroom environment. I started with better classroom control than I had at my last assignment. This proved to be beneficial throughout my experience. On my first day of teaching, I was very firm, direct, and self-confident. I set up the ground rules, grading system, and my expectations from the beginning. This was very important for classroom management over the next several weeks. Yet I faced a new problem of getting students to participate openly.

To deal with the problem of participation in my first-period class (tenth-grade American History), I set up several alternative work plans to ensure student comprehension of discussion materials. Students took notes, read out loud in class, and took regular quizzes. I also made use of puzzles and a daily journal to reinforce my objectives. This class was a lower level general class, and unless pushed constantly, the students did not initiate efforts to learn.

Motivation was a problem for all of my tenth-grade American History classes. In order to have any effect on these students, I had to be more creative than in the past. I needed to be selective when choosing class activities to stay within the time constraints set up by my co-op. I decided to use a cooperative learning activity that involved group work; outlining; research; and in several cases, creativity. I had the classes form groups of two or three students. They then chose a president and completed a research paper, using a choice of diagram, flowchart, outline, or bulletin board to describe that president. They shared their projects with the rest of the class. I was very pleased with the outcome.

Another creative activity incorporated into my lessons involved making a time line. These students had great difficulty with chronological order. Many of them had trouble visualizing differences in eras and sequencing events such as the election of President John Quincy Adams, the Civil War, and Prohibition. Students created a time line that showed the events we studied and other events in history relevant to individual students, including the formation of the band the Grateful Dead.

Student comprehension was enhanced when I used examples relevant to student experiences, for example, comparing an argument over who would buy a pizza for Friday night's party to the bad feelings shared among Great Britain, France, and the United States during the late 1700s and early 1800s. This drew students' interest because we were not just discussing "some old guys from history," we were discussing pizza.

I faced another problem with my psychology classes. I had only ever had three psychology classes in my life, and the last one was over five years ago. To teach this class, I completed more research than was required in any of my college classes. I learned the information, but I taught it using cooperative activities on an almost daily basis. This kept the students interested and allowed them to learn from one another.

At Utopian, my negative experiences all led to positive experiences. What I felt would be my problems (e.g., discipline, interest, knowledge of the subject matter) turned out to be my assets (e.g., class control, activities, cooperative learning).

My two teaching experiences were educational and rewarding, yet both were very different. The students, schools, and cooperating teachers were all different. Brookfield was a school of about 600 students, most of whom lived in a small, conservative town. The classes ranged in size from 14 to 22 students. Most of the teachers at Brookfield were young (under 40), and discipline was not a priority.

Utopian, on the other hand, had a student body of approximately 1,500. The students resided in rural, small-town, and urban settings. My classes ranged from 25 to 35 students. The teachers were mostly older and veterans of teaching. Discipline was very important at Utopian, and it was evident in the students' behavior and respect for teachers.

Student teaching turned out to be a rewarding, educational, and confidence-building experience. It increased my awareness of the problems faced by new teachers. I am unaware of all the problems I might face, but I am more confident that I can work through them and enjoy teaching. I learned that teaching was the appropriate career choice for myself and that I can successfully contribute to students' education. I did not realize how attached I would become to the students. I saw my students for only 50 minutes a day for eight weeks, yet I miss all of them. Surprisingly, the students who caused the most discipline problems are the students I miss the most.

Case Study 4:

My Experiences as a Student Teacher in Sweet Child Care Center and New Valley Elementary School

Tami

Case Study 4

Recently, I graduated from Bloomsburg University with a bachelor's degree in Elementary Education. As a graduation requirement, I student taught for 16 weeks in two different school settings. My placements were at Sweet Child Care Center and at New Valley Elementary School. During both experiences, I strengthened many of my teaching skills.

My first student teaching experience began at Sweet Child in January 1995. The center consisted of approximately 75 young children ranging in age from five weeks to five years. The children were grouped into three different age groups, and I spent the greatest amount of time working with the oldest group of children. My youngest student was three, and the oldest was five.

I spent the first couple of days getting to know the children and my coworkers. Everyone at the center treated me with respect and tried to help me feel like part of the group. The children were all wonderful. They couldn't wait until I arrived in the morning and would sit as close as possible to me throughout the day. One of the things I found most rewarding about working with these young children is that they constantly want attention and are so easy to love.

The most important quality needed to work with young children is the ability to gain their trust. At first, it is quite difficult to establish trust. The children loved to play with me, but they still went to my co-op when they were hurt or needed help. I was determined to gain trust from the children, and I wanted them to come to me for help and reassurance.

After ten days and a great deal of effort, I had my first very rewarding experience with a child. My co-op had the day off, and Ellexis, a little girl that came to the center only two days a week, arrived with her mother. She was crying and screaming because she didn't want her mother to leave. Her mother was late for work, and she didn't have time to calm Ellexis. I was left with a screaming child! After five minutes, much patience, and kind words, I reassured Ellexis that her mother would be back.

Shortly after I completed my second week, I realized the meaning of the word *patience*. These cute and loving children required 100 percent of my attention at all times. My co-op was not the sole teacher anymore, and the respect that I had wanted to gain was mine. But I wasn't expecting all the responsibility that came with earning their respect.

When I told people that I was student teaching in a day-care center, they would say, "Oh, you went to school to be a baby-sitter." Most people do not realize the amount of stress involved with teaching young children. I was responsible for 12 tiny lives for nine hours a day. Most people do not think that 12 children is a large number. I would agree, if the children were nine or ten years old, but 12 three- and four-year-olds is a lot for one teacher.

Children need help to do everything. Teaching one or two children requires a great deal of attention, but 12 young children require all of your attention and time-management skills. Managing time is essential in teaching children of this age. I had to spend an equal amount of time with all the children. State laws allow a ratio of 12 students to one teacher. Therefore, one teacher can have no more than 12 preschool-aged children at a time. When I was teaching a lesson, I was teaching a group of 12.

The attention span of a four-year-old is only about ten minutes. It was necessary to have many short activities planned throughout the day. The most effective teaching strategies were hands-on activities, songs, finger plays, and small-group activities. Children of this age need many visual aids and objects to keep their attention. They love to use their senses to learn.

While teaching at Sweet Child, I found myself spending most of my time disciplining children. Devin, an emotionally violent and unstable child, required special attention. A psychologist came to visit him twice a week. Devin would be sitting by himself playing with cars and then walk over and kick another child for no apparent reason. If Devin saw a toy that he wanted, he would hit and kick to get the toy. I was warned about him from my first day at the center. He had already hit and kicked my co-op several times. Working with a child like Devin was very challenging, but I feel that it helped me to be more alert in a classroom.

The first half of my assignment quickly ended. It was time to say good-bye to the children that I had been teaching for eight weeks. These children had made me laugh and cry, but more important, they had taught me the rewards of working with young children and the amount of love needed by this age group.

My next assignment took me to a third-grade class at New Valley Elementary School. A few weeks before my second assignment, I arranged a meeting with my new cooperating teacher. I was more nervous about starting my second teaching experience. Sweet Child was very challenging, but I feel more comfortable teaching younger children. I wasn't sure how the older children would accept my teaching techniques.

My first week of teaching went great! The students asked many personal questions. They were very curious about my life. My co-op had warned me to come on strict with the class so they would know I meant business. At first the class thought I was going to be a pushover, but they soon realized that I had the same expectations as their other teachers.

The most challenging problem was keeping the class on task. They were so interested in my presence that they kept interrupting class to ask personal questions. Trying to utilize this interest, I started a new game with the class. If they participated and kept on task during class time, I would answer three personal questions at the end of each lesson. This idea worked well for about a week. After a week, they grew tired of the game and knew almost everything about me. The children discovered that I could speak some Spanish, so I adapted the same game. If the class participated, I would teach them a few Spanish words at the end of each class. Teaching the children was not as difficult as controlling the classroom. My classroom consisted of 23 energetic students. Although it was difficult, I was thankful to have the freedom to develop my own rules and consequences.

My second week of teaching didn't run as smoothly as the previous week. When I would stop talking, the class would start to talk. I spent a great deal of time telling the class to listen, and this was taking away from my teaching time. I needed to find a method of keeping the students under control. After trying many different approaches, I finally found one that worked. The students loved their recess time, so I used this to gain classroom control. When the students would start to talk while I was teaching, I wouldn't raise my voice or lose my temper. I would calmly look up at the clock. The class would notice this and quickly get quiet. I would be looking at the clock and counting seconds. Each second counted was a second of recess time that they would lose. I found this method to work extremely well with this age group.

While at New Valley, my most challenging experience was with a girl named Crystal. Crystal was having a tough time with school and had been struggling all year. She had already failed a grade once. Retention was not an answer for her. She needed a special learning environment with smaller classes. Special arrangements were planned for the following year, but I had to work very hard to help her with the present school year.

Crystal would get 30 percents on tests and not even seem concerned. She was very frustrated with the system, and I needed to develop activities to help her remain interested in school. I shortened her spelling lists to allow her to concentrate on fewer words and help improve her grades. I wanted her to improve her grades and in turn improve her attitude about herself and school.

Crystal and I struggled for the first couple of weeks because she was satisfied with her failing grades and didn't want to do the work. She discovered that I was not going to let her turn in blank papers or rush through tests, and she became angry and resented my efforts. After about two weeks and many arguments, she finally started to come around. I shortened her assignments, but I made her redo assignments until she worked to her full potential. I tried to develop fun activities so learning was not viewed as a hassle for her. By the time I left New Valley, her grades and efforts in spelling and social studies had improved. After 16 weeks, my student teaching experience came to an end. I feel fortunate because I had the chance to work with the oldest and the youngest students in my field. Both experiences were challenging yet very rewarding.

The difference between the two placements wasn't the children but the school setting. Sweet Child is privately owned, and New Valley is part of a public school district. At the day care, I was responsible for a sick child, and for the rest of my class, until the child's parents arrived. In a public school, I could send the child to the nurse and continue with my lesson.

Another difference was the curriculum. At Sweet Child, I developed my own curriculum. I could spend a whole week discussing wind with the children, but at New Valley I was on a tight schedule. I had to teach an entire chapter about air, water, and temperature in six days. It was difficult to include experiments and activities on such a tight schedule. We used team teaching at New Valley; therefore, all third-grade classes had to follow the same schedule.

Perhaps the greatest difference in the two schools was the physical and emotional relationship expressed between students and teachers. At Sweet Child, we were encouraged to make the children feel loved. The children wanted kisses and hugs before they went home and throughout the day. Holding the children and giving them hugs were essential to make them feel secure in their surroundings. In public school, there is no touching at all. I showed affection by using facial expressions and writing nice notes on the students' papers.

After completing my student teaching experiences, I realized that one lesson remains consistent for all ages and grades of children: If an individual is interested in teaching, he or she needs to possess a love for children. The patience and trust of children for a teacher will develop over time, but the teacher's love of children must come from within. Teachers need the ability to forgive and forget. Every day ends, and it is important to leave problems behind and to start each new day with a smile.

Case Study 5:

My Experiences as a Student Teacher in Brookfield Area Middle School and Warwick High School

Brent

Case Study 5

I student taught during the winter season, when the weather was at its worst. As a result, I had to be prepared to alter my plans on short notice. While student teaching at Brookfield Area Middle School, the schedule changed almost every other day because of snow delay and early dismissal, in addition to typical eighth-grade interruptions such as achievement testing and high school orientation. I came to appreciate the fact that I taught the same course six times a day because it meant that I had to reorganize only one course when the schedule changed.

The school itself had a wonderful environment. All the teachers seemed to get along very well, and the students generally respected authority. The school relied on a team-teaching strategy that I found to be very effective. For example, when the schedule changed, there would often be gaps of time that needed to be filled. Invariably, one of the teachers would produce a videotape that could be shown to the entire team to fill the time gap. The videotape played over the school's closed-circuit television system and would come on only in the classrooms of a specific team.

From a technological standpoint, the school was not terribly advanced. Overhead and filmstrip projectors were easily obtained, but getting a VCR for an individual room was difficult. Apparently, this was not a high priority with the closed-circuit system in place. The system was so convenient that teachers tended to rely on it, often creating scheduling conflicts. One creative touch was that the morning announcements were conducted live each day by students over the television system. (I would love the opportunity to supervise students in that type of activity. The potential for creating a real student news program is fantastic.)

Brookfield students were very well behaved. During my first few weeks, I was amazed at how rarely the students needed to be disciplined. Most of the problems were easily corrected and very minor. If the situation became worse, the students went to in-house suspension. However, this punishment was often too extreme for a given offense, and there were no disciplinary provisions for students who broke small rules on a daily basis. As a result, the teachers designed a new disciplinary policy while I was there. Under the new system, minor infractions could result in a 15-minute detention period either before or after school. Failure to attend two detentions would result in in-house suspension. Under this system, the teachers could conduct day-to-day discipline without having to refer every student to the principal's office. This was important because the principal kept track of the number of referrals made by each teacher and because the teachers often felt that the principal was not sufficiently strict.

Overall, I found Brookfield to be a great place to teach. This came as a surprise because I had heard negative things about the district before my arrival. The teachers were professional and friendly, the students well-behaved and respectful, and the parents as involved as could be expected. My only difficulties were in dealing with schedule changes and in making sure materials were prepared ahead of time to ensure that support teachers could create adapted versions for inclusion students.

My second placement, at Warwick High School, offered a completely different experience. To begin with, I taught four grade levels instead of one, and three different courses each day. This put my time in very short supply. To further complicate matters, teachers could not touch the school copier. This meant that everything had to be prepared well in advance, and there was little room for last-minute changes to plans.

During my stay at the high school, teacher morale was extremely low, as the district was in the middle of contract negotiations. Loud arguments among teachers, and teachers not speaking to one another were common. Fortunately, I earned the respect of the faculty and was able to get along with everyone. Still, the atmosphere in the building was not ideal for student teaching.

Perhaps the best feature of the school was the incredible amount of technological supplies available to teachers. While there was no closed-circuit television system, there were VCRs, laser disk video players, and computers in every room of the science wing. In fact, it was sometimes difficult to move around the classroom because it was so cluttered with equipment. Nevertheless, I valued such hardware and used it regularly to enhance my lessons.

The highlight of the experience was dealing with the students themselves. Warwick is a rural school district, and I could identify some distinct characteristics shared by all students. They tended to be especially friendly, exceptionally tolerant of one another, and genuinely respectful of teachers. By using humor, developing interesting lessons, and showing the students that I enjoyed their company, I gained their respect and developed an excellent rapport. One of the best compliments I received was that many students were upset when I had to leave at the end of my placement.

My primary difficulty at Warwick was dealing with some of the upper-class students who did not want to be there. Their goal was simply to make it to graduation, and the day-to-day intricacies of science were of no importance to them. Adding to this difficulty, my cooperating teacher often allowed students great freedom to talk and get off task. I was uncomfortable with a lax classroom environment. It required determination, but I demanded the students' attention, and they responded better than I had expected. To be successful, I took an entirely different approach than I had used in the past. My lessons stressed less theory and relied on action and intrigue every single day. Flashy demonstrations and laboratory exercises were the only activities that captured the students' attention. While these lessons required more preparation, I found that the class was more fun to teach as well.

In retrospect, student teaching was a very positive experience. I was lucky to work in two entirely different situations, and it was encouraging to have been successful at both schools. I received some wonderful insights and compliments from the teachers, and I enjoyed excellent relationships with the students. Classroom management was not a problem. I feel very fortunate because I personally observed several student teachers who enjoyed none of these successes. I was able to overcome the minor problems. More important, I enjoyed myself. I truly miss the students. These are perhaps the most encouraging indicators that I have chosen the proper career.

Student-centered Learning/Library research project. Courtesy: Central Columbia Middle School.

Case Study 6:

My Experiences as a Student Teacher in Utopian Area High School and East Utopian Junior High School

Charles

Case Study 6

Student teaching in the Utopian Area School District was truly a learning experience. What my cooperating teachers and other faculty members taught me and my time spent in the classroom have definitely prepared me to become a classroom instructor.

My first assignment ran from mid-January to mid-March 1995 at Utopian Area High School. My cooperating teacher taught five periods of American History each day, a required class for a high school diploma in Pennsylvania. His schedule included hall duty, in which he policed the hall and boys' bathroom to prevent problems while classes were changing. When I arrived in January, the students were preparing for their second-quarter exams, so I did not begin teaching until well into the second week of my placement. Once the exams were completed, returned, and reviewed, it was my turn. For three days I taught two periods a day and added two more the following week. Therefore, my class schedule encompassed a total of four periods, 120 students per day, five days a week for the rest of the assignment.

The first class was rough, and I thought it was a total failure. My voice was monotone, I hid behind the desk, and the students sat and stared at me for the period. Needless to say, I went home upset and confused. Wasn't this easy? Couldn't anyone stand up and be a teacher? The answer is no, and if anyone will say otherwise, let him go into a classroom and try to teach 30 sophomores, and I guarantee he will change his mind.

My cooperating teacher was the reason I returned the next day, and for that matter, the entire first week. He reassured me that it would get easier if I moved around, used inflection in my voice, and varied my presentation to keep students interested. I did what he suggested, and my job became much easier; it even became fun. I opened up to the students, and they did the same. The days passed quickly, and soon it was time to give my first exam.

Creating a test was my next challenge, but again my co-op made this challenge easier. He showed me how to give a fair, comprehensive test using the materials given to the students throughout the chapter. The results were not as good as expected, but faculty members assured me that the grades adequately reflected student performance.

The most rewarding challenge that I was given at Utopian Area High School involved an opportunity presented by my co-op. I was able to teach another class, but with a twist: I had the freedom to use any type of instruction that I desired. What was also a change about this class was that it was at the end of the day and there were only ten students enrolled. This was a breath of fresh air after four periods of the same instruction. This was my chance to have full control. I turned a teacher-centered class into a student-centered classroom where the students read materials and then discussed the main points of interest. In effect, they became their own teachers, while I was there to supervise, answer questions, and interject my thoughts as needed. I regret that this experiment started late in the experience, for I did not have enough time to accomplish all of my goals before my placement ended.

I learned a great deal in the eight weeks I spent at Utopian Area High School. I learned what it is to be a teacher and the responsibilities that come with the job. All that I learned would not have been possible without the support from my co-op. The assignment would have been a failure without his daily advice. I hope all cooperating teachers are willing to help as much as he did.

From there, I moved ten blocks to East Utopian Junior High School. I was assigned to a good friend of my first co-op. Initially, I was apprehensive about moving from tenth to seventh grade. I worried about changing subjects. My specialty is history, and during my second placement, I was going to teach Civics, a course that I never had in school myself. However, my greatest concern involved my relationship with my new co-op. I had to meet a new teacher with a different philosophy.

I could not wait to start teaching. So on the second day, I started teaching two of my co-op's four Civics classes, picking up the full course load the following week. I kept this schedule for the remaining seven weeks, which passed very quickly. During my stay at East Utopian, I grew closer to the faculty than I had at the high school. Perhaps their age had something to do with it. Most teachers in the Utopian School District begin at the junior high level and later progress to the high school level. Therefore, most of the faculty consisted of fairly recent college graduates. The relative closeness in age meant that I shared interests with several other teachers. These teachers provided useful advice because they had been student teachers themselves not so long ago. I wish that I could have had a closer relationship with the teachers at the high school.

I was glad that I had a junior high assignment after the upper-level experience, because the difference between the two is astounding. My sophomores often seemed to be uninterested, even after I adapted teaching styles and varied my presentations. The seventh-grade students were the exact opposite. They were always interested, even with material that seemed difficult for their age. They were inquisitive and asked about many "what if" situations. The idea of teaching the seventh grade scared me at first, but the change was actually good, because I worked with more motivated students in my second placement.

The second assignment provided several experiences that I did not encounter at the high school level. At East Utopian, daily bus and lunch duties entailed supervising the kids at the worst times of the day: when they are still half asleep, and when they are hungry. During these duties I witnessed fights, spitting, throwing food, and the other great habits of junior high students. All student teachers should experience lunch duty to see the other side of their students! I also had the opportunity to substitute for the homeroom teachers and other faculty members who were away during emergencies. I learned what it meant to be a substitute with unfamiliar students. It's not the best job in the world. As an Algebra I substitute, everything went well, considering that seven years had passed since I had taken Algebra I.

Again, the assignment was successful thanks to my cooperating teacher. Worrying about changing co-ops was unnecessary. I got along well with each co-op. Both individuals were excellent role models, and I hope I will be half as good as they are at their work. These teachers are assets to the Utopian School District. My co-op at East Utopian was willing to help at any time and gave me the freedom to teach in my manner. He became my friend, not just co-op, for the experience. That made a difference.

The experience flew by, and soon the weather began to break. I discovered another phenomenon that every student teacher needs to experience: *spring fever.* One day they pay attention, the next day they are preoccupied with the nice weather. Even the teacher finds it hard to concentrate when the weather changes. I was glad when May 11 rolled around and I was free to enjoy the upcoming summer. May 11, 1995, also marked the end of my stay at Utopia. I was glad about my placement there for my student teaching, and I hope that future placements with these two fine teachers will continue to benefit others.

Case Study 7:

My Experiences as a Student Teacher in Nubalm Elementary School and Utopian Area Elementary School

Meghan

Case Study 7

There are many responsibilities, deadlines, and schedules to become accustomed to when approaching your first student teaching assignment. I often fantasized about having a text or guide that I could refer to with all of my doubts. A book entitled *Everything and Anything You Ever Wanted to Know About Student Teaching* would have been helpful. The amount of lesson planning, the physical fatigue, and the art of evaluating a lesson are only a few things I wish I had been aware of before student teaching began. I hope that these reflections on my successes and difficulties will assist other students in knowing what to expect on their journey into teaching.

As it does for many student teachers, my anticipation for meeting my supervisor and my cooperating teacher, and entering the classroom, grew as the semester approached. I spoke to the co-op for my first assignment on the telephone days before the end of the fall semester. We spoke about her specific requirements, arrival time, the size of the classroom, and the subject content I would be teaching.

Unfortunately, the name of my supervisor continued to be a mystery until the day of Student Teaching Orientation. The orientation was scheduled to begin at 9:00 A.M. Student teachers and supervisors were to gather and discuss requirements for each teaching assignment. Unfortunately, an abundance of snow delayed students and supervisors and prevented the orientation from starting on time. The orientation turned out to be a reunion for classmates who had made it though the snow. At least I knew my supervisor's name.

The anticipation continued, and so did the snow. Schools remained closed for the rest of that week. By January 21, the elementary school was open, and the rural streets were finally cleared. Mixed feelings emerged. I was quite nervous, excited, and worried. I worried most about the overall impression I would make. I had constant thoughts of How do I look? Do I look professional? Do I seem too enthusiastic? Finally those feelings calmed as I began to interact with the second graders.

Most student teachers observe lessons for a period of time up to one week. My cooperating teacher advised me to take on a subject when I felt comfortable with the environment. It was personally important that I observe the whole classroom. This included my co-op's teaching style, her classroom management approach, the physical attributes of the learning environment, the length of lessons, and the transition from one lesson to another. It was very helpful to observe students' behavior before, during, and after lessons. I continuously observed the students' level of participation as well as verbal responses throughout different lessons. This proved beneficial while preparing lessons throughout my teaching assignments.

The lack of cooperative learning in the classroom inspired my idea for my first lesson. Throughout many lessons that I observed, the students remained seated in rows. I respected my cooperating teacher's methods, but I wanted to explore my own teaching style.

My first lesson was a positive experience with some negative results as well. I designed a spelling lesson as a game. I constructed a word scrambler using the week's spelling words. The students formed four teams, and each team received a piece of paper to write out the scrambled word. An hourglass served as a timing device. I was organized, and the directions were clear. The lesson began when I turned the hourglass and revealed the scrambled letters. Students watched the hourglass intently, and whispers of "Hurry, Hurry" filled the classroom. Time ran out, and the winning team wrote the word correctly on the word scrambler board. As the second and third turn ended, students were yelling "Hurry," reaching for the hourglass to save time, and calling one another names. At that moment, I knew I would continue most lessons with the students seated at their desks arranged in rows. Cooperative learning was something I wanted to practice, but it is quite difficult to change a classroom's teaching environment on a short-term basis. This lesson temporarily changed my views about cooperative learning.

Only a week later, I prepared a math unit that used a flannel board. Lessons required hands-on activities and cooperative learning. While the unit was a huge success, I encountered some minor problems with classroom management.

My cooperating teacher used seating arrangements and her teaching style as classroom management tools. I wanted a more tangible and instantaneous method to gain classroom control. I needed to control the noise. I did not want a permanently quiet classroom, nor did I want to have to tell the second graders to be quiet.

To deal with classroom noise, I created a simple "2-Cue" technique ("2" standing for second graders). I explained the reasoning of this technique to the class: Although I liked to give them time to talk, talking often grew too loud, and we needed a quiet class while explaining directions and while others were still working. So when I wanted quiet, I would write a large 2 with a red marker on the 2-Cue box that I had created.

When the 2 appeared on the box, students would be penalized for speaking without permission. If the children talked or outwardly misbehaved when the 2 appeared, I dropped small 2's into the box. For every 2 dropped into the box, the class lost recess or learning-station time.

The second graders developed certain responses as I wrote the large 2. As I started at the top and curved down the figure, students would grunt, hum, or whine. Their responses grew louder as I reached the bottom of the figure. Silence filled the classroom at the very second my marker lifted from that box.

It requires a great amount of time to plan most lessons. Some lessons took hours to develop. During my time at Nubalm Elementary, each grade occupied one classroom, and an additional wing was being built. This new wing would include a library, which was nonexistent during my time teaching there. The absence of a library created a shortage of teaching materials such as books, maps, bulletin boards, and media resources. This situation made planning more difficult but expanded my creativity. As materials were not available, it was up to the teachers to create the entire learning environment.

My cooperating teacher opened her classroom to experimentation. In other words, she wanted to see how I would create a learning environment. By the end of the eight weeks, the classroom contained a variety of learning stations, bulletin boards, and a reading corner. Each of these was valuable in assessing the effectiveness of my lessons and measuring students' interest in the activities.

Beginning a new assignment can bring out some of the same anxieties experienced during your first assignment. For my second assignment, student teaching at Utopian Area Elementary School, I prepared myself for a hectic schedule. For this assignment, I commuted from Bloomsburg daily, and I enjoyed the lengthy drive. It gave me time to ponder lesson plans and daily events.

I allowed more time to observe the sixth-grade classroom. Many adjustments would occur during this transition from a primary to an intermediate grade level. While observing the students and my cooperating teacher, I noticed the respect between the teacher and the students. I hoped that I too would gain that respect from the students.

The well-organized classroom displayed a list of student jobs, contained various media resources, and positioned desks in orderly groups. A steady pace was kept throughout the day. As I spent more time teaching at Utopian Elementary, I noticed that this pace resulted from using every moment wisely. If one lesson ended early, the next lesson would shortly begin; there were no time lapses. My cooperating teacher's time-management style increased class control. Timing and modifying lessons were difficult tasks at first. Many of my lessons ended too quickly, allowing students to read or whisper for three to four minutes. This situation invited problems. I began to plan in advance for lessons, and I eventually mastered classroom timing. I often found myself remembering my own sixth-grade experiences where the teacher was inept in lesson pacing and time management. Remembering such experiences helped me gain a realistic view of student behavior.

Initially I used the chalkboard for brainstorming and writing information. At that time, the desks were arranged in a U-shape, with three connecting rows. During one science lesson, I was noting many diagrams and definitions on the chalkboard. Each time I turned to face the students, those seated in the last row would quickly sit down. This happened a few more times, and the students quietly chuckled each time. I was eager to find out what preoccupied the sly sixth graders, so I purposely dropped my chalk. Behind me, I discovered 24 students performing "the wave." A variety of media resources, including the overhead projector, helped me control some classroom behavior. From that moment on, I no longer turned my back to the students.

Student participation and verbal responses determined the upcoming activities. In one social studies lesson, we had just completed a unit on the French Revolution. I finished my lesson plan, but I was having difficulty finding an activity that would physically involve my sixth-grade class. During prior lessons, I had used maps, the game Jeopardy, and group research papers. It was time for all students to participate, even if they were not called on or did not volunteer.

That night I drove to campus to visit one of my professors. I explained my challenge, and we discussed my goals and ideas for that particular lesson. We spoke of classroom management and the materials I could use to eliminate chaos during my lesson. That night we brainstormed, and I gathered helpful hints to involve the entire class.

Later that evening, while looking over my ideas, I created a simple lesson that would physically involve all students. While planning this lesson, I considered the students' prior subject knowledge, the time of day the lesson would take place, and methods to maintain class control without using my voice.

The lesson began by handing each student a large card that contained an important event of the French Revolution. I distributed cards face down on desks, and the students were not to look at their cards. Directions appeared on the board and were orally reinforced. At the appropriate time, all sixth graders were to stand up holding their cards, and without speaking to one another, they were to arrange the cards (events) in chronological order. The lesson took time, but the students remembered the events later, because of the colorful cards and the teamwork required to construct the time line of events.

My teaching assignments were different in many aspects, but each day my confidence in teaching grew. My lessons improved daily because of student feedback. Whether it was a verbal response or a behavior during a lesson, student responses helped me to evaluate my lessons and my teaching style. As my own critic, I used these responses to evaluate my teaching progress.

Student teaching is a wonderful yet challenging experience. It is your opportunity to experiment with the lessons and theories you have created and studied. Each experience is an opportunity to challenge your doubts and to turn difficulties into successes.

Chapter 4

ℰᏩᏃ

Common Student Teaching Problems and How to Deal With Them

Although student teachers undertake truly unique teaching experiences, the problems they encounter are often similar. Most student teachers will openly admit they were unsure of what to expect during student teaching. Upon first entering the classroom, student teachers lack clear understanding of teacher responsibilities and performance expectations.

Veenman (1984) has identified 24 common problems of beginning (first-year) teachers, including maintaining classroom discipline, motivating students, dealing with individual differences among students, assessing student work, dealing with parents, organizing class work, coping with insufficient materials and supplies, and dealing with problems of individual students. Although Veenman's 24 common problems are similar to those presented throughout the case studies, this book discusses seven major problems experienced by student teachers. They are assuming the teaching role, establishing a professional relationship with students, coping with lengthy preparation time, pacing lessons and units, dealing with failed expectations, motivating students, and managing the classroom.

These seven problems were the ones most frequently identified by almost 200 student teachers surveyed at Bloomsburg University between

1991 and 1995. Although these were the most common problems, other difficulties alluded to in the different case studies are also significant.

Getting Started

Unsure of what to expect, most student teachers enter the classroom with feelings of anxiety, nervousness, and inadequacy. Meeting a cooperating teacher, meeting students, and becoming familiar with school policies and subject matter can be overwhelming. Many student teachers are apprehensive about their first placements, and the initial anxiety often returns during the second placement. Student teachers experience the stress of entering a new career and evaluating their career choice. Nervousness is common and perfectly normal. Prior to the beginning of a placement, there are several steps that student teachers can take to help relieve anxiety.

Student teachers need to seriously consider getting started before they begin their student teaching. They should contact their cooperating teacher soon after learning his or her name to arrange a meeting at least a week before a placement begins. This will give student teachers a chance to meet their cooperating teacher and ask questions about her/his expectations; see their classroom and resources; ask questions; get copies of needed classroom textbooks; and collect information about school policies and procedures. A cooperating teacher will most likely be using a planning period to meet a new student teacher. As a courtesy, student teachers should prepare questions ahead of time. If possible, student teachers should plan to spend an entire day at the school. This will allow them to become familiar with school grounds, meet colleagues and school administrators, and observe the student body.

Another important aspect of getting started is meeting with the college supervisor and learning his or her expectations. To a great extent, knowing about the college supervisor's expectations can be helpful in relieving the anxiety and nervousness that often accompany a supervisor's arrival at the school for a lesson observation.

In most teacher education institutions, student teaching is considered a course, and it is graded accordingly as pass/fail or on a scale of A to E. As a result, college supervisors expect student teachers to meet certain requirements and demonstrate mastery of some competencies to be awarded a passing grade. Therefore, student teachers should endeavor to learn course requirements, expected competencies, and grading policies.

Chapter seven discusses in detail what most college supervisors require of student teachers and what they look for during lesson observations. Although these requirements are supposed to be addressed at the student teaching orientation, there is a need for constant clarification of them by the college supervisor. Lack of constant communication among student teachers, cooperating teachers, and college supervisors can also create anxiety and uncertainty for students. It is important that there be an opportunity for frequent dialogue between the student teacher and the college supervisor. All of these actions help student teachers to relieve nervousness and form a more accurate idea of what to expect while student teaching.

Establishing a Professional Role

Establishing a professional relationship with faculty and students is essential to a positive student teaching experience. The anxiety of getting started often leads to apprehension and a general lack of assertiveness. As the case studies in chapter 3 show, student teachers are concerned about establishing mutual respect and trust with their students.

One student teacher, Diann (case study 3), expected an automatic transfer of student respect from her cooperating teacher to herself. Her expectations promptly vanished, and she is quick to admit that she regrets being overly friendly with students at the beginning of her placement. This friendliness and an initial lack of aggressive classroom management strategies led to many disciplinary problems that could have otherwise been avoided. Similarly, in case study 1, Christy points out that she actually had to learn to say No to unreasonable student requests.

Generally, establishing a professional role in a school setting involves the student teacher's behavior, awareness, and preparation. Most of the student teachers reported success with establishing a professional role. Apprehension was overcome with time, and mutual respect was established through firmness and fairness.

Preparation

Preparation is especially difficult for student teachers, for while they are preparing they are continually learning. The scope of preparation includes adjusting to long hours of planning, searching for teaching materials, learning or relearning subject matter, varying presentations, creating and grading tests, and critiquing one's own performance.

Adjusting to the long hours of preparation can be troublesome for beginning student teachers. Most new teachers are amazed that lessons can require hours of planning each day. Once student teachers have found materials and activities, they must compose the lesson. Creativity, motivation, and content are all considered during planning. In the case studies, student teachers reported lesson plans to be the most time-consuming component of preparation.After creating the lessons, some student teachers (such as Brent in case study 5 and Meghan in case study 7) mentioned difficulties with obtaining needed teaching aids and equipment.

Student teachers then attempt to create a test appropriate for student ability levels and reflective of classroom learning experiences. Test construction and grading are also time-consuming parts of preparation. Needless to say, student teachers reported experiencing a general lack of free time.

Preparation begins with planning lesson units. Lesson units focus on broad themes and follow subject curriculum guides and sequential learning activities. Lesson units usually span periods of time ranging from one week to one month, but they vary in length depending on the depth of study and the content. Through unit planning, teachers create a clear purpose and focus for daily teaching activities because daily lesson plans serve as components of a broader lesson unit.

Although composing a formal lesson plan for each lesson can be time-consuming, lesson plans play a vital role in achieving success while teaching. Each component of a formal lesson plan serves as an organizational tool devised to help ensure effective teaching. Lesson plans keep teachers and students focused and on task during a lesson. They clearly outline lesson materials and content and the teacher's lesson expectations.

There are many different lesson plan formats. Madeline Hunter's format, for example, is highly recommended to preservice teachers by teacher educators. Her design includes a lesson preview, a daily instructional goal, performance objectives, an initiation activity, content (new terms, facts, and concepts), instructional strategies, closure, evaluation techniques, a list of materials needed for the lesson, and a bibliography (Olrich et al., 1994). Following in the next few pages are outline of a lesson unit and lesson plan, sample lesson plan format describing each subheading and component parts of the lesson plan, and two examples of lesson plans, for third and seventh grades.

Classroom Management: Monitoring and keeping students on lesson task.
Courtesy: Berwick Area Middle School.

Outline of a Lesson Unit

<u>Unit Title</u>:
<u>Course Title</u>:
<u>School</u>:
<u>Teacher's name</u>:
<u>Grade Level / Class Description</u>:

<u>Unit's Instructional Goal</u>:

<u>Rationale</u>:

<u>Unit Preview</u>:

<u>Unit Performance Objectives</u>:

<u>Unit Content</u>:

<u>Unit Instructional Strategies</u>:

<u>Unit Evaluation</u>:

<u>Unit Outline</u>:

<u>Outline of a Lesson Plan</u>

<u>Lesson Title</u>:
<u>Grade Level</u>:
<u>Teacher's Name</u>:

<u>Lesson Preview</u>:

<u>Instructional Goal</u>:

<u>Performance Objectives</u>:

<u>Initiation Activity</u>:

<u>Content</u>:

<u>Instructional Strategies</u>:

<u>Closure</u>:

<u>Evaluation</u>:

<u>Materials and Resources</u>:

<u>Bibliography</u>:

Lesson Plan Format

Lesson Title:
Grade Level:
Teacher's name:

Lesson Preview:

The lesson preview identifies what student experiences the lesson is intended to convey. This consists of a detailed but brief lesson topic description.

Instructional Goal:

One goal should be the focus of a daily lesson. This goal ensures that the teacher is focused and has direction for the lesson. The goal should be stated in terms of student understanding and behavior. Performance objectives should reflect the lesson's instructional goal.

Performance Objectives:

Two to three objectives are reasonably obtained within a class lesson period of 45 minutes. Performance objectives should be clearly stated in terms of observable student behavior. These objectives help to ensure that teacher expectations are met and that tests reflect student learning experiences. Three essential elements create a performance objective: the condition, the performance statement (action), and the criterion.

The *condition* concerns the circumstances that must be present for students to satisfy the lesson objective. Examples of condition statements are "using a globe, with the aid of a dictionary," or "using notes and from memory." The *performance statement* should be stated in observable terms using an action verb, e.g., "identify," "summarize," "define," "outline," or "add." The *criterion* expresses the minimum level of accuracy necessary to satisfy the objective. Examples range from "with complete accuracy" to "nine out of ten questions will be answered correctly."

Initiation Activity:

This is a motivation device used to develop interest in the day's lesson. This activity presents the significance and importance of the lesson by relating the new topic to previously learned material and areas of student experience or interest. An initiation activity may consist of showing a filmstrip, relating an anecdote, reading a short story, asking open-ended questions, and completing various other activities. However, this activity should contain a direct link to the lesson content, and it should never be used solely for student entertainment.

Content:

Any new terms, facts, concepts, or generalizations presented during the lesson should be listed here. This provides content focus and highlights new learning material. Many teachers also use the lesson plan content section for notes and a brief presentation outline.

Instructional Strategies:

Instructional strategies concern how you will teach the lesson. Basically, these strategies include any means of teaching or instruction used during a lesson. Lecture, questioning strategies, deduction and induction, class discussion, group activities, simulation, games, direct instruction, and cooperative learning are a few of the teaching strategies that could be listed in this section. Also to be included is a brief outline or description of the content of the lesson. During lecture, a teacher can occasionally refer to this note to ensure that she or he is on the right track. Moreover, this section should clearly state student as well as teacher activities. If the students should be taking notes during a lecture, this should be indicated. Anticipating student activities allows a teacher to easily recognize unacceptable student behavior.

Closure:

Closure brings continuity to any lesson or unit. This part of the lesson summarizes the purpose and content of the daily activities. During closure, the teacher backs off and assumes a less dominant role. The teacher asks questions on the lesson taught and clarifies aspects not clearly understood by students. Closure is an occasion where students inform the teacher of what they have learned during the lesson and how this material relates to their world or previously learned information. The teacher may ask directed questions to prompt student response, but the teacher should not summarize the material for students. Closure cannot successfully add continuity to a lesson without student participation.

Evaluation:

Each lesson should include some type of evaluation. Evaluations may consist of formal tests and quizzes or informal strategies. Oral or written questions, student summaries of a lesson, and homework assignments can evaluate student understanding.

Materials and Resources:

Books, posters, videos, filmstrips, audiocassettes, tests and quizzes, student handouts, audiovisual equipment, and any teacher or student supplies needed for the daily lesson should be listed. This section serves as an organizational tool. Listing materials needed for each daily lesson ensures that a teacher is prepared and has obtained needed teaching aids.

Bibliography:

List any source used to compose the lesson. This is an important item to include in your formal lesson plan. If any content material of your lesson is disputed, you can easily refer others to your source. Including a bibliography helps illustrate the amount of preparation put into the lesson. It also shows your level of research and the outside material you have brought in to supplement the class textbook. In addition, the bibliography also helps a teacher identify outdated materials and author or time-period bias, and it serves as a reference for future lessons.

Completed Lesson Plan #1

Lesson Title: The Food Groups

Grade Level: Third Grade

Teacher's Name: Jody

Lesson Preview: This lesson will introduce students to the different types of food.

Instructional Goals: The students will understand that food can be sorted into six main groups.

Performance Objectives:
1. After the class picnic, the students will name each of the six food groups.
2. During the picnic, the students will discuss the different types of food they like to eat.
3. After the lesson, the students will be able to give three examples of the food found in each food group.

Initiation Activity: Tell the students we are doing a very special activity today. We are going to have a class picnic. If weather permits, take the class outside to a safe area. If not, do this activity where there is plenty of space. Spread out the blankets to sit on and bring along the picnic basket. The children will be filled with excitement!

Content:
- Food Groups
- Bread, Cereal, Rice, and Pasta Group
- Vegetable Group
- Fruit Group
- Meat, Poultry, Fish, Dry Beans, and Nuts Group
- Milk, Yogurt, and Cheese Group
- Fats, Oils, and Sweets Group

Instructional Strategies:
1. After spreading out the blankets, show students what they brought along for the picnic. Some items you may want to include are apple slices, orange wedges, cheese, pretzels, cereal, peanuts, candy, carrots, hard-boiled eggs, etc. Be sure the children are not allergic to any of the foods at the picnic. Prior to this activity, send a letter home to the parents informing them of this activity and asking for volunteers to supply food.
2. Explain to the class that we are going to talk about the six different food groups.
3. Encourage the class to sort the food according to the different food groups.
4. The teacher will point out the six main food groups and use their proper names.
5. After the food has been sorted, allow the students to sample the food with one another. Encourage discussion among the students.
6. In their Nutrition Journal, students will draw pictures of some of their favorite foods under each food group.

Closure : Ask students questions about the food groups. Elaborate on aspects that need further clarification.

Evaluation: The teacher will observe the students writing in their Nutrition Journal. If a child needs further explanation, the teacher will provide additional help.

Materials and Resources:
- blankets
- picnic baskets
- paper plates
- napkins
- apple slices
- orange wedges
- cheese
- pretzels

- cereal
- peanuts
- candy, etc.
- NOTE: Be sure to include examples of food from each food
  group.

Bibliography:
This activity was adapted from Mrs. Jane Doe, a first-grade teacher at
Utopian Elementary School.

Completed Lesson Plan #2

Lesson Title: The American Party System
Grade Level: Civics Grade 7
Teacher's Name: Christy

Lesson Preview:

This lesson provides students with background information about the formation of the two major American political parties and the current role and structure of American political parties.

Instructional Goal:

Students will develop an understanding of the historical impact of political parties.

Performance Objectives:

1. Using lecture notes, students will be able to accurately compare and contrast the different histories of the Democratic and Republican Parties.
2. Using a class handout, students will be able to accurately present political information in a bar graph.

Initiation Activity:

Questioning strategies will determine student knowledge of the origins of the Democratic and Republican parties. Open-ended questions and a display of teacher-created visual aids will be used to create interest in the formation of the American two-party political system.

Content:

Anti-Federalist, Federalist, Democratic party, Democrat, Republican party, Republican, Abraham Lincoln, Andrew Jackson, partisan, independent party.

Instructional Strategies:

Lecture, questioning, and limited class discussion will be used to present essential textbook material. A series of teacher-made visual aids will be used in combination with lecture techniques. Students are currently learning the Cornell method of note taking and may be given class time to revise and maintain their subject matter notes. Students will be given a handout and time to work, alone or in groups, to complete a bar graph. Historical information about American political parties will be presented. Along with textbook material, essential skills such as taking good notes and presenting material in a graph form will be stressed.

Closure:

Students will recall the major points discussed in the course of the lecture and group assignment.

Evaluation:

Evaluation of student mastery of subject matter terminology will be determined through a short matching quiz. Class discussion and teacher questioning will ensure that students have an accurate understanding of the history of American political parties. Completion of a bar graph and in-class teacher review of graphs will ensure that students are able to present information in a graph form.

Materials and Resources:

- Teacher-made posters of the history of American political parties.
- Teacher-made vocabulary quiz.
- Classroom Textbook pages 149-154.
- Student Handout: "Understanding Visual Elements-Creating a Bar Graph" (Teacher's edition textbook supplement)

Bibliography:

Bowes, John, Cathryn Long, Elizabeth Lott, and Mary Jane Turner. 1990. *Civics: Citizens in Action.* Columbus, Ohio: Merrill Publishing Company.

Clearly, a formal lesson plan is a teacher's daily schedule for a unit of teaching material. It keeps the teacher organized, focused, and prepared. A lesson plan can eliminate many last-minute instructional difficulties. It also allows others to take over a teacher's classes in case of a scheduled or unscheduled absence.

Pacing Activities and Lessons

Almost all of the student teachers in the prior case studies (Christy, Tami, Brent, Charles, Meghan) mentioned problems with pacing. The amount of time to allot to a unit, a lesson, or an activity is often hard to predict. Daily interruptions, classroom distractions, and changes in the weather led to difficulties with the pace of teaching. Lack of student understanding, availability of teaching resources, and class participation were also frequent pace disrupters. Initially, many student teachers found predicting the pace of lessons to be difficult.

In her first placement, Christy (case study 1) was terror stricken by her inability to predict the amount of time needed for specific activities. For the first few days, her lessons ran counter to her time-frame expectations, leaving her with extra time or not enough time to complete planned activities. Increased teaching efficiency was also a problem. A lesson that took 50 minutes to complete in a morning class only lasted 30 minutes in the afternoon. In her second placement, Christy found herself teaching and reteaching lessons to ensure student understanding.

Meghan (case study 7) not only experienced problems with the timing, modification, and transition of lessons, she also needed to make several adjustments because of student behavior. Other student teachers experienced similar difficulties. In case study 5, Brent experienced the difficulty of altering plans because of frequent schedule changes brought on by the winter weather. Charles (case study 6) mentions the difficulties of presenting lessons when both the students and he have been stricken with "spring fever."

All of the aforementioned student teachers admitted that their difficulties with pacing eased with time and flexibility. Their suggestions for mastering the pace of learning and for successful time management include breaking activities down into 15- to 20-minute intervals, planning flexibility, and overpreparation. Extra time is a dangerous element in the classroom, and it can be avoided only by adequate planning. Planning one or two extra activities should combat the problems created by a faster-than-expected pace.

Student Performance vs. Teacher Expectations

The high expectations of student teachers are often shattered at the completion of the first exam. Student teachers wonder if they have tested what they taught or if the test was adequate for the student ability level. Christy (case study 1) and Charles (case study 6) actually questioned their ability to teach after reviewing the results of their first test.

The case studies also present advice that may help student teachers form reasonable student performance expectations. Seeking counsel from a cooperating teacher and other colleagues may put a student teacher's mind at ease. Student teachers should seek a frame of reference for student achievement. They should consider offering more comprehensive test reviews and adapt tests for ability levels but not become defeated. Above all, they should continue to hold high expectations, for this often motivates students to achieve.

Motivation

Whether student teachers are trying to motivate an entire class or specific low achievers, developing effective motivation techniques can be challenging. Making lessons interesting, fun, and meaningful to students is sometimes difficult, and time constraints often limit creative activities. Students, at any level, may see little relevance in learning certain subject matter. It may be difficult to instill the desire to perform to full potential for particular students or classes as a whole. In case study 3, Diann experienced motivation problems with all of her tenth-grade American History classes. Increased teacher creativity and required class participation improved the learning atmosphere.

Tami (case 4), Brent (case 5), and Christy (case 1) experienced the problem of motivating students who possessed little desire to be in school. Tami adjusted lessons and requirements for a low-achieving student to allow this student to build self-confidence. Brent relied on flashy demonstrations, and Christy referred a failing student to the school administration. Motivating this student, who refused to care or respond to motivation techniques, proved to be too difficult a problem for Christy to handle on a short-term basis.

Motivation is an important tool for both students and teachers, and it serves academic as well as practical purposes. Students perform to academic potential if they are motivated to learn. Equally important, teachers enjoy teaching during time that may have otherwise been spent keeping students on task.

Several motivation techniques can be used during a lesson. Motivation techniques can be related to subject content, student interests and experiences, or student desire for achievement. The simplest and most effective motivation techniques involve helping students to recognize their full academic potential. This can easily be achieved through establishing a good rapport with students and through effective use of praise.

According to Morganett (1995), the quality of student-teacher relationships is a crucial variable in eliminating disruptive behaviors from the classroom. He suggests ten methods for improving student-teacher relationships and establishing a good rapport with students:

1. Get to know students by name as quickly as possible.
2. Get to know some personal things about each student.
3. Conduct a values analysis about some current event or topic.
4. Provide positive comments when appropriate.
5. Be positive and enthusiastic about teaching.
6. Show students that you are not only interested in them but also that you care about them.
7. Avoid the use of threats and punishment.
8. Do not play favorites.
9. Create a supportive classroom environment.
10. Create an environment where questions and answers—even wrong answers—are encouraged and valued.

In the *Vocational Education Journal*, Sullivan and Wircenski (1988) discuss various methods for motivating students. Many of their suggestions overlap the motivation techniques suggested by Morganett (Morganett, 1995). Some of their suggestions are highlighted on the following pages.

1. Know your students and their names as often as possible.
2. Set your room in a U shape to encourage interaction among students.
3. Send lots of positive messages with posters, bulletin boards, and pictures.

4. Vary your instructional strategies: Use illustrated lectures, demonstrations, discussions, computers, tutoring, coaching, and more.
5. Review the class objective each day. Be sure the students see how the entire program moves along.
6. Make your instruction relevant. Be sure your students see how the content relates to them and the world of work.
7. Open each presentation with an introduction that captures the interest of your students.
8. Be expressive with your face—SMILE!
9. Put some excitement into your speech; vary your pitch, volume, and rate.
10. Use demonstrative movements of the head, arms, and hands; keep your hands out of your pockets.
11. Use words that are highly descriptive; give lots of examples.
12. Accept students' ideas and comments, even if they are wrong; correct in a positive manner.
13. Maintain eye contact and move toward your students as you interact with them; be sure to nod your head to show you are hearing what they say.
14. Give lots of positive feedback when students respond, offer their ideas, perform a task correctly, come to class on time, and bring their materials to class.
15. Use appropriate humor in your teaching and in tests, to relieve anxiety.
16. Provide opportunities for students to speak to the class.
17. Return assignments and tests to students ASAP. Be sure to make positive suggestions and comments.
18. Teach by asking lots of questions during introductions, presentations, demonstrations, and laboratory work.
19. Be aware of those students requiring assistance, and then see that they get it.
20. Be consistent in your treatment of students.
21. Plan relevant study trips out of the school.
22. Bring dynamic subject matter experts into your classroom.
23. Recognize appropriate behavior and reward it on a continuing basis. Praise students in front of the class; reprimand them in private.
24. Use games and simulations to spark interest, provide a break in the routine, and supplement a unit in your curriculum.

Student praise is surely a key element of motivation; however, many teachers fall into the pattern of praising with a few overused and all-too-common statements. Students like a variety of feedback responses. A statement such as "good job" may be an effective praise statement when used judiciously, but if overused, "good job" might limit positive student reactions. A few alternative praise suggestions are listed on the following page.

Sullivan and Wircenski (1988) suggest the following praise comments:

1. You're on the right track.
2. You did a lot of work today.
3. That's absolutely correct.
4. Great work!
5. That's the best you've ever done!
6. Good thinking.
7. You're doing a super job!
8. Congratulations.
9. I think you've got it now.
10. Fantastic!
11. You remembered!
12. Terrific!
13. How did you ever think of that?
14. That's a neat idea.
15. Perfect!
16. You're really improving.
17. Outstanding!
18. Way to go!
19. Way to wrap it up.
20. I'm proud of you.

Classroom Management

Overall, the most common problem mentioned by student teachers is classroom management. Establishing an effective classroom management policy early in a placement is a key element in achieving success during that placement. A frequently mentioned difficulty involved keeping classes on task and dealing with off-task behavior. Chronic talking, passing or writing notes, and general inattentiveness were the most common forms of off-task behavior reported by student teachers.

The elementary education student teachers, Tami (case study 4) and Meghan (case study 7), dealt with these problems in a much different manner than the secondary education student teachers. Tami attempted to bribe the students with Spanish lessons. When this method lost the desired effect, she relied on a system of clock watching. Each lost second of class time resulted in a corresponding loss of recess time. Meghan created the "2-Cue" system to eliminate off-task talking. Essentially, this system also resulted in a loss of recess time for undesirable behaviors.

The secondary teachers often used subtle ways of deterring unwanted behavior. In case study 5, Brent prevented off-task behavior with his own increased creativity. Flashy demonstrations and intriguing classroom presentations allowed little time or reason for off-task student behavior. In her first placement, Christy (case study 1) combated off-task behavior with body language, frequent classroom movements, seating chart adjustments, and subtle comments. More serious behavior offenders were approached during class for a quiet and private chat. At the junior high level, body language proved ineffective. Many students were unaware that body language was being used. These students were kept on task by a daily review of classroom procedures and rules.

In case study 3, Diann experienced a more serious classroom management problem. Initially, she was very friendly and not assertive enough with student disciplinary matters. This led to many disciplinary problems that might have been easily avoided if she had been firmer from the beginning. She spent the entire placement trying to regain control of her classes and experienced limited success in doing so. Although she regained control of most of her classes, some students remained a problem and she failed to regain control of one class altogether.

Diann's methods to regain control included a behavior point system, whereby students lost points from their class participation grade when they displayed disruptive behavior. She also used her body, locating herself near disruptive students. Finally, if behavior was not adapted, she would announce their names and request an end to their behavior, or she would pull them aside to talk about their behavior.

Using common sense, adapting your own teaching behavior, and forming realistic expectations about student behavior may solve many classroom management problems. In case study 7, Meghan experienced a problem pertaining to use of the chalkboard. Students would perform "the wave" when she turned her back to the class. This was easily solved. She refused to turn her back to the students for the remainder of the placement.

A common problem for student teachers involves ignoring classroom management theories stressed during their methods courses. This is not usually an intentional act on the part of student teachers. They are simply overwhelmed with the details of their teaching and tend to react to students with the first classroom management strategy that comes to mind. Unfortunately, a great deal of planning and thought are required to implement classroom management theories. This is not always recognized by student teachers. Student teachers also need to experiment with different classroom management theories to determine which methods work best for them and for their students.

Examining all the case studies presented makes clear that student teachers could have dealt with classroom management problems more effectively if they had used strategies learned during methods courses. In particular, they needed to relate theory to practice. Various research-based theories have been proven to be effective classroom management strategies; however, these strategies are seldom implemented in student teacher classrooms, as indicated by the previous case studies. Effective strategies include desist, reality therapy, assertive discipline, and behavior modification. It would be helpful at this juncture to briefly examine these contemporary classroom disciplinary strategies.

Desist strategy is perhaps the most immediate teacher reaction to student misbehavior. Jacob S. Kounin and Paul V. Gump (1959) developed the desist strategy for teacher-student communication. The strategy requires teachers to develop a systematic means of informing students that their behavior should change. This communication could be a signal, a glance, movement around the room, an action, or a comment. There are two types of communication, public and private. For the majority of cases, such as if a student is talking, a private, low-level command is the best strategy to use. In contrast, an incident like a classroom fight requires a public, high-level command. Another aspect of the desist strategy is the level of force. There are three levels: low, moderate, and high (for further explanation, see table 1). The low level of force is usually nonverbal, e.g., glancing at a disruptive child, or moving over and standing close to the student while you are speaking. Since no one likes others to encroach on his or her space, the disruptive student will feel threatened and naturally change the behavior. This technique has been found to be extremely effective in correcting a misbehavior. Moderate force is verbal (however, yelling at a student is inappropriate). Simply tell the student to stop the behavior or remove the distracting objects. A high level of force is usually verbal and nonverbal. An example could include removing the child from the group or physically restraining him or her in a way that is not harmful. A private display of force is not meant to be noticed by the entire class, but it can be discernible to the students surrounding the misbehaving student. A public display of force should be noted by almost every student in the class. For instance, a public force would be telling a student in an authoritative tone of voice to stop the disruptive

Table 1
Illustrations of Desist Strategies

Level of Force	Definition	Desist Strategy
Low	Nonverbal, a signal or movement	Glancing at child, shaking head, moving over to child unobtrusively in the instructional activity
Moderate	Verbal, conversational, no coercion	Appealing to child to act reasonably, removing disturbing objects, commanding the child to stop
High	Verbal and nonverbal, changed voice pitch, may use coercion	Raising voice & commanding child to stop, removing child from group, threatening, punishing, physically restraining the child
Type	**Definition**	**Desist Strategy**
Public	Intended to be noticed by most of the children in a class	Acting and speaking in a way that commands attention
Private	Intended to be noticed by small groups of children	Using unobtrusive actions or moving close to a child when speaking

Source: Wallen, Carl J., 1968 (January), *Establishing Teaching Principles in the Area of Classroom Management* (Interim Report, Project No. 5-0916), Monmouth, Oreg.: Teaching Research, Appendix A, p. 15. In Orlich, Donald C. et al., 1998, *Teaching Strategies: A Guide to Better Instruction*, 5th ed., Boston: Houghton Mifflin, p. 201.

action. However, it should be noted that there is a disadvantage to the use of public force. In a 1970 study, Kounin noted that a "ripple effect" occurred as students in a class went off task or were adversely affected as they observed a teacher confronting a disruptive student.

The desist strategy also stresses student involvement in the establishment of classroom rules. Students should be told the consequences of a disruptive behavior, and they should be helped to enforce the rule. In many schools, taking away certain privileges such as recess or extracurricular activities is common. Corporal punishment is sometimes used, but it is increasingly becoming unlawful and less popular. Most school districts have a policy concerning corporal punishment. Suspensions and expulsions are other forms of punishment that could be considered in desist strategy. These options are usually handled by the school principal.

Reality therapy allows students to take responsibility for their actions. William Glasser (1965) maintains that reality therapy leads all people toward reality, toward grappling successfully with the many aspects of the real world. Essentially, reality therapy is responsibility training. Students evaluate their own behavior, and if it is unacceptable, they determine more acceptable alternatives. Reality therapy is based on a number of principles. One important principle is human involvement. The teacher must strive to develop good rapport with students to give them the confidence or self-esteem they need to enter into a lasting professional relationship with either the teacher or others. The existence of a professional relationship between a teacher and a student can become effective in the resolution of a classroom management problem. Another principle of reality therapy is the need to focus on the student's current behavior—what the student is doing now. Teachers should always ask the student *what he or she is doing now*. This question encourages the student to examine his or her current behavior and to judge for himself or herself that the behavior is inappropriate. Also, there is the principle that the teacher should help the student develop plans to change an inappropriate behavior. Furthermore, the student must show a genuine commitment to implement the plan. This commitment could be in a form of a written contract. Another important principle is that there are no excuses for failure to change an inappropriate behavior, especially when a student has made a commitment. When failure occurs, it should be recognized that the responsibility lies with the student. Above all, there is the final principle, which says there is no punishment in reality therapy. Glasser believes that punishment destroys student-teacher involvement and has not been proven to be effective in reducing classroom discipline problems. Although the above principles of reality therapy are usually applied to individuals, reality therapy can also be effectively used for an entire class during class discussions.

Assertive discipline is a no-nonsense approach to classroom discipline. Assertive discipline empowers the teacher to take charge of the classroom and the student to be responsible for his or her actions. Assertive discipline was developed by Lee and Marlene Canter (1988). It evolved in response to the increasing discipline problems in today's public schools. According to the Canters (1992), students of today are much different from students of the past. Students today are bringing more than pens and pencils to school. In increasing numbers, they're bringing with them the confusion and uncertainties of broken homes, poverty, emotional and physical neglect and abuse, and the fact of life that too many of their parents are unwilling or unable to motivate them to succeed in school. Thus, schools today are no longer conducive for learning. Most inner-city schools have been taken over by gangs and drug dealers. Teachers are intimidated and physically and verbally assaulted. This leads to a situation where many students cannot learn.

Therefore, to be effective, the teacher has to be assertive. Lee and Marlene Canter point out that an assertive teacher is "one who clearly and firmly communicates her expectations to her students, and is prepared to reinforce her words with appropriate action. She responds to students in a manner that maximizes her potential to get her own needs to teach met, but in no way violates the best interest of the students" (1992, p. 14). An important element of assertive discipline is helping teachers learn how to establish and implement rules that prevent behavior problems from occurring. It is equally important to empower students to make responsible decisions about their behavior. In assertive discipline, there has to be evidence of a commitment by both the teacher and the student. Basically, for a teacher to be effective using assertive discipline, she must (1) establish rules for encouraging appropriate behaviors, (2) outline the types of behaviors that are expected, (3) outline behaviors that are unacceptable, (4) identify consequences or punishment for unacceptable behaviors, (5) be firm and consistent in enforcing the rules, and (6) be willing to seek support from the school principal, instructional supervisors, guidance counselors, and parents.

Behavior modification is based on B. F. Skinner's (1953, 1954) behaviorist psychological theory. Cangelosi (1993) notes that behavior modification refers to the approach by which students' environments are manipulated to increase the chances of desirable behaviors being rewarded, while undesirable behaviors go unrewarded. In other words, behavior modification strategy is a system that uses reinforcement for good behavior and punishment for bad behavior. The strategy involves charting student behaviors to determine and change the causes of undesired behavior.

This strategy requires observation and time. Behaviors cannot be immediately deterred, for finding the cause may take some investigating. While this approach does not show immediate results, it allows teachers to eliminate the causes of future misbehavior. Examples of behavior modification in a classroom include adjusting seating, taking away recess, and withdrawing other privileges for a disruptive student. When behavior modification is adopted in a classroom, it is also necessary to recognize and reward positive behaviors. To accentuate positive behaviors, teachers often use tangible rewards such as candy, stickers, gifts, praise, or nonverbal compliments such as smiling, giving thumbs-up signals, and nodding approval.

Any of these strategies can be effectively used during student teaching. Student teachers may even use these approaches without being aware of the method they are using. Student teachers should experiment with various classroom management styles to determine what works best for them and for their students. They should also keep in mind that altering their own behavior may also eliminate classroom disruptions.

All the common student teaching problems are directly or indirectly related to one another. Lesson plan components such as evaluation and closure may help a teacher with the planning and pacing of future lessons. Effective motivation and teacher preparation may prevent extensive need for classroom management time. In turn, developing effective classroom management policies can improve student–teacher rapport and student achievement. The components of teaching are all interrelated. Therefore, it is important to systematically consider how teaching problems may be resolved through alterations of teacher and student behavior in the various aspects of classroom learning.

Chapter 5

℘⒭

Teaching in a Block Scheduled School

Block scheduling is a recent phenomenon in the organization of the duration of lessons in public schools across the country. Block scheduling or intensive scheduling is a learner-centered school improvement initiative popularized by Dr. Joseph Carroll. It is the process of lengthening the class period from forty-five minutes to about ninety minutes. Canady and Rettig (1996) note it is the process of organizing time into longer instructional periods to enhance teaching and learning potential. Block scheduling evolved in response to the criticism that the regular forty-five minutes class period is not enough for teachers to present instructional materials in sufficient detail or for students to adequately spend time interacting with content. It has also been pointed out that instruction is fragmented for students in the traditional classroom schedule. As a result, schools districts have collapsed classroom instruction from the usual eight periods a day to four. Klein (1998) describes the schedule at Fox Chapel Area High School as consisting of four eighty minute periods that meet each day. Furthermore, she notes that most courses were scheduled for a semester block plus two additional periods during the other semester. There was also a thirty minutes activity time at the beginning of each school day (p. 28). Basically, teachers would have students for a course for ninety days in a semester instead of one hundred and eighty days. A significant characteristics of block scheduling is that you can no longer expect to teach the same quantity of material as in a regular forty-five minutes lesson. Moreover, block scheduling compels you to teach using a topical approach instead of a chronological approach. You teach content in more detail and therefore, student retention should be better.

Although there seems to be a great deal of benefits in block scheduling, teachers have expressed some concerns over the adoption of block scheduling. In an interview with master teachers in a large school district in Pennsylvania, the teachers' concerns were identified to include what teachers will be doing for the entire eighty-six minutes?, where are teachers going to get the instructional materials, audio-visual, and other equipment to use for eighty-six minutes class period?, what can teachers do to keep a low level academic students on task for eighty-six minutes?, etc. Indeed, student teachers equally have to wrestle with these concerns. An additional issue for the student teachers can be, what would happen if a lesson runs short of the class period?, will she/he be able to control the class when students become disruptive?. College supervisors will often find that these are legitimate concerns. Student teachers usually have problem with time management. Lessons run short of the scheduled forty-five minutes class period, leaving time for students to become disruptive. With the current trend toward a eighty-six minutes class period, student teachers will certainly experience more problems as illustrated in the narrative below (vignette 1) by a student teacher who compared his experiences teaching in the traditional classroom scheduled school and a block scheduled school.

Vignette 1
Experiences of a Student Teacher in a Block Scheduled School
By Gregory

Perhaps nothing is more frightening than being placed in a block scheduled school. As students and student teachers, we are constantly preparing for the regular "run-of-the-mill" forty minutes period. We make our lessons so that they fill the forty to forty-five minutes allotted to the period. In a block scheduled period, the class time is divided into eighty to eighty-six minute blocks. This might cause some great amount of panic while imagining oneself teaching during this entire time. This is more true when one's first placement is in a school with the traditional class schedule.

I first student taught eight grade in a regular period; forty minutes long. Many of the materials that I was to teach were pre-existing, and all that I had to do was to put them into some kind of logical order and teach them. In addition, the teaching materials and equipment available to us were incredible: four computers with access to the Web, four televisions, three overheads, our own copier, LCD panel display, LCD projectors, a VCR connected to all of the televisions, even a stereo system. I think the word 'ideal' is an accurate description of this particular classroom.

When I went to my next placement, all of these wonderful tools were no longer at my disposal. On top of this fact, I had to teach for eighty-six minutes. I began to panic and wonder how in the world I would make my lesson go for this long amount of time without putting my students to sleep (or making myself insane). Obviously, simple lecture will never work for the duration of the period. One might face a class that simply refuses to stay awake.

I made the mistake of lecturing with student discussion randomly interspersed to the first of my class. They were ninth graders, twenty-two of whom had problems in school. I needed to find a way to teach my information in a creative and effective way. They could usually go no longer than fifteen minutes on a task that was not intrinsically motivating to them. I first had to establish an effective classroom management plan, because they could not handle any type of unstructured environment. Once I did that (with a classroom contract), I could begin to focus on things to do in the classroom. Worksheets, a few games, creative writing, and other activities I invented were used to break the time up. My cooperating teacher and I discussed the 'rule of three' which means creating at least three activities within a class period. The activities should be structured and should be creative as possible. This takes an incredible amount of creativity, an amount that I had to adjust to. Nothing is more frustrating than sitting down at night and thinking how am I going to teach this and having no clue where to begin.

In these classes, I needed more resources to work with. I think that if a school district is adopting block scheduling, the maximum number of tools should be available and provided to the teacher. I had neither access to a copier where I could run off copies, nor did I have access to supplementary materials. These difficulties made creating three activities per lesson a challenge, and sometimes, a pain. I had a book , my brain, and (occasionally) a computer. My cooperating teacher had to run to different offices to make copies, something that required a decent amount of time. I tried my best to get the work done the night before, but did not always accomplish this.

I could not just combine two lessons to create one lesson. First of all, the ideas must have a constant flow, one that is not always in two different lessons. The extra time allows one to move more quickly through materials and allows time to make activities that do not have to be stretched over a few days. Students can be presented with an uninterrupted flow of ideas. This is where the teacher's creativity comes in. The teacher must invent or use ideas that are new and different to teach the material. Eighty-six minutes class periods lend themselves well to activity. Depending on the dynamics of the class, anywhere from one to four activities can take place in one period. I also gave my ninth graders a break roughly half way through the period. This broke up the activities further, and allowed them to relax for few minutes (no more than eight). If one does not give them a break, they will take one whether one approves of it or not.

If a block scheduled school is where one gets a job or placement, do not panic. Solicit ideas from other teachers. Use the "rule of three". Be as creative as possible. Be flexible in the course of your lesson. Use hands-on learning activities to teach materials. Sometime the best idea is to explain for few minutes at the beginning of class and then let the students discover things on their own. As always, provide structure and support as they are working. Block scheduling has its own set of problems and concern, but also has unique advantages.

Indeed, the narrative above provides a useful insight about teaching in a block scheduled school. It is obvious that teaching is very challenging in a block scheduled school for either the teacher or the student teacher. In order to be effective in a block scheduled school it is advisable for teachers and student teachers to talk to other teachers in school districts which have already adopted block scheduling. Teachers can find information from colleagues in other school districts who are already doing it. A teacher in-service seminar would be an appropriate forum to explore questions about block scheduling.

The following are suggestions of instructional strategies which student teachers and teachers can implement in their classroom for an effective block scheduled lesson:

1.) Break down your instructional tasks and assign minutes to each task (e.g. present a fifteen to twenty minutes lecture on a content).
2.) Present a case study
3.) Set up cooperative learning groups to work for few minutes on a project.
4.) Show a portion of a video tape on the content to re-affirm what you have already taught.
5.) Use review games, simulation, debate, and role play. This is highly recommended in a social studies class.
6.) Ask students to write (e.g. write a journal on the content presented in the lesson, write an essay or evaluate the lesson that was presented). The use of more methods of evaluations will be beneficial at this juncture, and
7.) Leave room for feedback from students.

Students and teachers have a lot to gain when the school district adopts block scheduling. It enables the teachers to become more familiar with their students and therefore are able to determine their strength and weakness. It allows teachers to become more creative and to try new things that will work with each class. Teachers can become more excited as they are involved in the subject matter, and this can be passed on to the students. Beside, it affords teachers the opportunity to use teaching methods which normally can not be used in a forty-five minutes class period (e.g. debate, games, role play, and simulation). Klein (1998) personal experience with block scheduling corroborates our assumption.

She put her experiences succinctly "I must say that teaching for eighty straight minutes can be very exhausting...but I must also add that it can be very rewarding. I no longer have to compress a wonderful simulation into forty minutes, have a debate interrupted by the bell, or have the students leave with questions unanswered (p.29)". Moreover, block scheduling will enable teachers to prepare for the needs of slow learners in their classes. Reading assignment can be geared to the slow learner, and there is enough time to go over the assignments. The more things you can do and re-enforce it, the better it is with the slow learner. Besides, block schedule class period allows teachers to help students on how to do library research or a major project. There are also some benefits for the students. Because students are able to stay longer with the content, lessons can become fun if the learning experiences are properly arranged. Block scheduling has been found to be helpful in the improvement of students basic score in the Iowa Test of Achievement and Proficiency (klein,1998). Block schedule also gives students opportunity to get more courses. Students are able to enroll for more courses. For instance, students can enroll for eight courses a year instead of seven. For students going on to colleges and universities, it gives them opportunity to deal with materials in depth as in the universities.

Few disadvantages of block scheduling include, finding enough instructional materials to use for a lesson. Teachers need much larger quantity of instructional materials, e.g. handouts, worksheets, audio-visual materials, etc. Furthermore, due to the length of the class period, the last lesson of the day tends to be the most difficult because students are tired. Attention span is short, so teachers would need more activities in that class period. In other word, teachers would find that not all class periods are created equally in terms of teaching effectiveness and student academic achievement.

Chapter 6

ℰℐℭℛ

Teaching in an Inclusive and Culturally Diverse Classroom

With the increasing changes in the demographics of our society and school populations, teachers need to be prepared to design their instruction to suit the diverse learners in their classroom. The U.S. population is growing, and so are minority groups in the population. This change is rapidly becoming obvious in the nation's classrooms. For instance, according to the Statistical Abstract of the United States, the 1990 census, the U.S. population grew by 10 percent between 1980 and 1990, reaching a total of 249.8 million, an increase of 23 million people. Ninety percent of the 23-million-person increase occurred in the southern, western, and eastern states, such as New York and New Jersey. Three states accounted for almost half of the nation's growth: Texas, Florida, and California increased their populations by a total of 11.7 million. According to Hodgkinson (1991), the census clearly shows that the states with the most population growth are those with a great deal of ethnic diversity. He notes that while the white population increased by 15 million, the nonwhite population increased by 14 million. Even though the numbers of whites grew by 8 percent, their share of the total U.S. population declined from 86 to 84 percent.

A culturally diverse classroom. Courtesy: Central Columbia Middle School.

Regarding projected changes in the nation's youth population for 1990 to 2010, Hodgkinson adds that "the nation will gain in total population, but America's youth population will decline rapidly after 2000. . . . However, as the total youth cohort moves from 64 million to 65 million, and then down to 62 million, the non-white component of the nation's youth cohort will increase dramatically from 30% in 1990 to 38% in 2010" (1991, p. 39). These figures have important implications for teacher education and classroom instruction. Teachers need to be trained differently, and instructions have to be prepared so that every child will be able to relate to them. Teachers have to be sensitive to ethnic and cultural diversity in their classrooms. Schools have to be willing to develop or introduce specialized programs such as multicultural education.

According to James A. Banks and Cherry A. McGee Banks (1997), multicultural education incorporates the idea that all students—regardless of their gender; social class; and ethnic, racial, or cultural characteristics— should have an equal opportunity to learn in school. He points out that some students, because of these characteristics, have a better chance to learn in schools as they are currently structured than do students who belong to other groups or who have different cultural characteristics. The goal of every teacher should be to ensure that every child is given equal opportunity to learn so that all children can have a good education. To attain this goal, teachers have to use a variety of instructional strategies.

Multicultural Lesson Tips

Because the traditional American public school curriculum emphasizes a Eurocentric perspective, teachers should endeavor to infuse ethnic content into their instruction. Multicultural lessons can effectively make every student in class develop a sense of self-esteem and feel welcomed and respected. Multicultural lessons enable students to develop not only a sense of cultural awareness but also knowledge, attitudes, and skills needed for survival in a democratic society. A good multicultural lesson must be broadly developed (content must be diversified and apply to multiethnic groups), interdisciplinary, and comparative; rely on concepts and generalizations, not facts alone; teach basic skills; and help youths to make reflective decisions (Banks, 1976).

In a culturally diverse classroom, teachers must also consider what Pang (1994) refers to as "unconscious prejudices," which can be expressed either by tone of voice or by use of terms such as "those" children, "them," and "us." Teachers must avoid showing prejudice or using stereotypes about any group. Indeed, teachers sometimes speak or behave in ways that limit the growth of their students. For example, in a culturally diverse classroom, a culturally naïve teacher may use the word "those children" to refer to black children or minority children. Moreover, teachers should avoid giving children from minority groups assignments that may reinforce existing stereotypes of their cultural group (e.g., asking a black student to do a research paper on athletics or about basketball). Teachers must endeavor to recognize and affirm cultural differences in a way that makes learning effective and meaningful.

The culturally diverse classroom can provide a great deal of opportunities for learning. Students learn in different styles. They learn from one another not only in the classroom during instruction but equally during interaction in the school hallway, on the play ground at recess, in the cafeteria during lunch, at the gymnasium, and even, daily on the bus as they ride to and from the school. On any of these occasions, the teacher should be proactive and assist in the creation of a positive and warm atmosphere where every student can socialize and learn from one another. There is no reason why a student should feel isolated in a school. Unfortunately, the reality is that a lot of students are isolated. There is "self segregation" in our educational institutions. There is rarely interracial socialization. Students can be seen interacting along racial background either on the school play ground during recess or in the cafeteria during lunch. This can be traumatizing for a young child who is not familiar with discrimination. For instance, there was a six-year-old son of an African immigrant who complained to his parents few weeks after they moved into a suburban school and neighborhood in northeast Pennsylvania that his classmates often refuse to play with him during recess. In tears, the child narrates his experiences in the school, pointing out that he feels "isolated and out of place". Teachers should not allow this situation in their classroom. Teachers can intervene if students cannot socialize on their own across racial differences. We live in a global society and teachers must create in students the awareness of cultural differences and how these differences contribute toward making our society unique. The teacher must give every student, whether of a different racial or religious background, a chance to learn and acquire a sense of empowerment and efficacy. These conditions are essential for academic achievement.

The Inclusive Classroom

We have emphasized the need for teachers to recognize the racial differences of students in their classrooms and to use these differences in enhancing learning and student self-esteem. In the same manner, there is a need to recognize children with special needs in our classrooms. American society has yet to deal with the issue of handicapped, or special-needs, children in schools, just as it has yet to deal completely with how to teach children of different racial backgrounds. In American schools today, there are different categories of children with special needs. There are those with physical disabilities as well as those with learning and emotional disabilities. In most cases, little effort is made in teacher education programs to train future teachers in how to handle students with these disabilities in the classroom. Additionally, problems created for preservice teachers as a result of mainstreaming these special-needs children into the regular classroom are often overlooked by veteran teachers and school administrators. For instance, many different specialists apart from the principal teacher are now commonly seen in classrooms. As a result, classrooms today are like a "road show" with many experts (teacher's aids, sign-language interpreters, etc.) coming and going. This makes the role of a student teacher in an inclusive class more complex and challenging, as described in the narrative below (vignette 2) of a student teacher.

Vignette 2
Experiences of a Student Teacher in an Inclusive Classroom by Christopher

One difficulty that many student teachers face during their student teaching experience is making adaptations for students with special needs. While attending my university, I had many courses that prepared me to write lesson plans and create interesting and thought-provoking activities for lessons. However, I had only one class that provided me with any information about how to accommodate special-needs students. The class, Introduction to Exceptional Individuals, was only an introductory course mainly designed to help preservice teachers identify problems and to explain the characteristics of certain exceptionalities.

When I arrived at Brookfield High School, I did not expect to have students in my class that were blind, deaf, and suffering from spina bifida. In my first-period class, I had a student who was deaf. At first, I felt uncomfortable talking to him because it was hard for me to understand him, and I didn't like asking him to repeat things. I felt that this would draw attention to his exceptionality, make him feel uncomfortable, and cause him to disengage from the lesson. If he feared that he would not be understood, I reasoned, he might stop volunteering to answer questions.

In the classroom with Ben was an interpreter who translated my spoken words and those of the rest of the class into sign language. Before my first lesson, the interpreter came to me and asked me to speak at a normal pace and speak loudly enough so he could hear me when my back was turned away from him. At first I was nervous that I was speaking too quickly for the interpreter. Then I would worry that I was speaking too slowly for the rest of the class. Eventually, I chose a pace that seemed natural for me. This pace seemed to be fine throughout the rest of my placement. During my second week of teaching this class, I announced to the class that I would be showing a video. After class, the interpreter came to me and said that he would bring a closed-captioning machine into school with him. I had never seen one before. Usually they are built into the television. However, some of the televisions in school are old and do not have these features. When I turned on the television and the words began flashing across the bottom, I waited for another student to say, "Why are those words going across the bottom?" Nobody said a word.

On a couple of occasions, Ben got a little out of hand in the class and I had to tell him to calm himself down. It was rather unusual to be telling this to a student who couldn't hear you. The interpreter would have to translate the message to Ben because Ben would avoid eye contact with me when he decided to become involved in off-task behavior.

The narrative above underscores the need for student teachers to be better prepared for special-needs situations in today's classroom. Student teachers have to be able not only to develop adapted lessons but also to deal with students with behavior disorders. These skills are needed to be effective in an inclusive classroom.

The concept of inclusion is synonymous with the mainstreaming approach introduced in the 1970s to integrate children in special education classes with those in regular classes. Advocates of inclusion, however, think the concept is more comprehensive than mainstreaming. As Schmidt and Harriman (1998) have stated, full inclusion is an approach in which all students are in general education classrooms in their community schools, regardless of the nature or severity of their disabilities. Full inclusion is undergirded by the same philosophy as that of multicultural education: Every child in the community—irrespective of disabilities, race, gender, or religion–should have an equal opportunity to be educated.

The adoption of inclusive practice needs commitment not only from the school system but also from parents, the community, and higher education institutions. Teacher education institutions have to give student teachers skills supportive of inclusive practices. Students teachers should be able to recognize children with special needs. Students should be taught not to be afraid of interacting with or talking to other students in wheelchairs. Teachers can show a good example by not making a "big deal" of issues involving children with physical disabilities. Rosa Hernandez Sheets (1997) maintains that adult apprehensiveness about the topic only thwarts children's natural curiosity, reinforcing the confusion and fear children may feel when encountering differences they do not understand. And for children with special needs, the ignorance and insensitivity of others often leads to painful stereotyping and exclusion. It is naïve to believe that children do not recognize physical disabilities or racial differences in their peers. Studies by Derman-Sparks (1995) indicate that by age two, children begin to ask questions about unusual attributes such as absence of legs, as well as about special equipment and other markers of disability (e.g., crutches, wheelchairs, eye patches). At ages three and four, children want to know what people with disabilities can and cannot do. In a school district where inclusion is practiced, the teacher must preempt students from asking offensive questions by explaining the diversity in every one of us. As Sheets (Sheets, 1997, p. 130) has rightly pointed out, we all have unique characteristics and limitations (e.g., physical disability, vision difficulties, height and weight problems, etc.), and we cannot make them "go away" overnight or sometimes ever. Physical disabilities can also occur because of an accident resulting in permanent paralysis to our limbs and hands (e.g., spinal cord injuries). Unnecessary fear and anxiety by children can be put away if teachers explain to members of the class that there is no way to contract someone else's disability.

It would also be helpful if teachers would explain scientific and technological advances that have enabled physical and emotionally disabled individuals to live normal lives with little assistance from adult helpers. Teachers should provide illustrations of specialized equipment that has enabled physically disabled persons to live normal lives, e.g., prosthetics, wheelchairs, and canes for those with paralyzed limbs; braille machines and guide dogs for blind persons; sign language and hearing aids for those who are hearing impaired; and eyeglasses for those who have difficulty with vision. Children will be able to relate to and appreciate the experiences of individuals who use this equipment if, as a classroom activity, the teacher will put the children in groups and ask them to identify people in their family who have any of these physical disabilities. Within their groups, each child can take turns discussing how he or she has been helpful to the disabled persons in the family. This classroom activity helps foster empathy and understanding for people with disabilities.

Furthermore, it is necessary for the teacher to point out to students that children with disabilities have strengths, skills, and talent just as they themselves do. With this encouragement, children will learn to see those with disabilities as peers, not objects of pity (Sheets 1997). Additionally, it will be important to explain that every student in the class has individual needs and that the teacher will be fair in meeting those needs. This will remove undue attention from the disabled student when he or she is being helped by the teacher or a teacher's assistant. Students can also be encouraged to volunteer to help their peers who have physical disabilities.

In an inclusive classroom, the teacher's goal is to achieve educational equity. As Orlich et al. (1998, p. 328) have aptly stated, "Your job as a teacher is to ensure that all students have equal access to instruction and essential services, and that discrimination based on physical attributes and other characteristics is not tolerated". A teacher should assist students (physical or intellectually challenged) who are unble to interact with their peers, in getting into social and cooperative learning groups.

Chapter 7

৪৩৫২

Evaluating Student Teaching

S tudent teaching can be fun when student teachers know exactly what college supervisors and cooperating teachers are looking for during a lesson observation. Most teacher education institutions provide student teachers with a student teaching handbook, where teaching requirements, evaluation criteria, values, and descriptions are carefully explained. Prior to beginning their first assignment, student teachers should study the handbook and become familiar with its content.

Generally, upon observing a student teacher, college supervisors and cooperating teachers want to see how well (ranked from unsatisfactory to superior) a student teacher performs on the following criteria (Bloomsburg University, 1992):

1   Communication and Interaction Skills
   * English Usage, Oral
   * English Usage, Written
   * Effective Presentation of Ideas
   * Handwriting
   * Spelling
   * Voice
   * Promotion of Interaction

2 Teaching Atmosphere and Management
   - Class Control
   - Attitude Toward Students
   - Pupil Responsiveness
   - Creation of Positive Environment
   - Instructional Strategies
   - Management Strategies

3 Subject Matter, Knowledge, and Instruction
   - Mastery of Subject Matter
   - Selection of Appropriate Goals
   - Planning and Organizing of Lessons
   - Implementation of Lesson Plans
   - Use of Media and Resources
   - Degree of Flexibility
   - Imagination and Creativity
   - Application of Principles of Learning

4 Professional Attitudes
   - Interest in Self-Improvement
   - Acceptance of Criticism
   - Commitment to Teaching
   - Dependability and Promptness
   - Initiative
   - Enthusiasm
   - Poise and Self-Control
   - Relationships With Colleagues
   - Maintenance of Appropriate Records
   - Grooming and Dress

5 Assessment, Diagnosis, and Evaluation
   - Responsiveness to Student Development Needs
   - Educational Programs
   - Curricular Materials
   - Evaluation Methods and Materials
   - Professional Role
   - Community Expectations
   - School System Expectations
   - Performance Upon Feedback
   - Evaluation of Student Learning

It should be noted that the above model is by no means a standard instrument for all teacher education institutions. There may be variations depending on the emphasis of the individual institution. In addition, to facilitate teaching improvement, many college supervisors require student teachers to write unit lesson plans, keep a journal of reflection, develop a portfolio and bulletin boards, and videotape lessons. Nevertheless, this model provides an insight into what supervisors look for when a student teacher is presenting a lesson.

Chapter 8

℅℃

Evaluation Forms

Although schools and universities use different types of student teacher evaluation forms, definite similarities appear. Usually, there is the weekly student teaching observation (assessment) form, and the final evaluation form which is completed at the end of the student teaching assignment. Most forms evaluate the same components of the teaching atmosphere. For example, they include evaluations of the strengths and weaknesses of teachers and student teachers. Many forms also require evaluation of teaching strategies, classroom management, and topic materials. Most forms include a section for comments or suggestions for improvement. While most forms evaluate the same aspects of teaching, they can vary in their length, depth, and detail.

Examples of standard evaluation forms have been provided in this chapter to convey the similarities, differences, and topics discussed. The first form is utilized by faculty at the Ohio State University, College of Education, School of Teaching and Learning. The second and third form are excerpted from the Bloomsburg University (1992) *Student Teaching Handbook*. The fourth form presented has a much higher degree of detail and evaluates specific teacher behaviors, actions, and teaching performance. This form is currently in use at the Bloomsburg Area School District.

Form #1
Weekly Assessment for Pre-Service Teachers

Pre-Service Teacher's Name: _____

Field Professor: _____

School: _____

Date: _____

Rating Scale: 5 = Excellent, outstanding, 4 = Good, better than average, 3 = Fair, average, 2 = Poor, less than average, needs considerable improvement, 1 = Unacceptable, N/A = non-applicable.

Goal One: Pre-teaching Interaction and Behaviors

1. _____ Pre-Service Teacher interacts well with students. Shows interest and engagement. Comments:
2. _____ Demonstrates a positive and professional attitude with students and teachers. Comments:
3. _____ Models teacher behavior (as opposed to student behaviors). Comments:
4. _____ Demonstrates commitment to becoming a professional teacher. Works to improve and develop skills. Comments:
5. _____ Asks questions of "how" and "why" to other teachers about teaching styles, methods, lessons, content, etc. Comments:

Goal Two: Instructional Planning

1. _____ Demonstrates knowledge and skills in the instructional planning of units and lessons. Comments:
2. _____ Infuses global and multicultural perspectives. Comments:
3. _____ Deals maturely with controversial issues. Comments:
4. _____ Finds and uses diverse instructional resources. Comments:
5. _____ Uses knowledge of K-12 scope and sequence, and of the graded course of study. Comments:
6. _____ Recognizes his or her own biases, limitations, etc. Works toward correcting, changing, and understanding them. Comments:
7. _____ Aware when something isn't working and moves to change it. Aware if students are off task and seeks ways to reinvolve them. Comments:

(continued)

Goal Three: Instructional Methods

1. _____   Uses a variety of instructional methods that encourage active learning. Comments:
2. _____   Meets the need of different learning styles in their students. Comments:
3. _____   Methods agree with and meet educational goals and content. Comments:
4. _____   Meets the needs of their students' various abilities. Modifies as needed. Comments:
5. _____   Teaching strategies have students actively find, process, use, and examine many different perspectives. Comments:
6. _____   Leads a discussion to get students thinking about, articulating, and evaluating what they are learning. Comments:
7. _____   Flexible in transitions and in modifying lesson plans. Comments:

Goal Four: Student-centered Focus

1. _____   Demonstrates awareness and support of students as individuals and learners. Comments:
2. _____   Builds rapport with and respects all students. Comments:
3. _____   Seeks out information about students.   Learns students' knowledge base, background, problems, interests, etc. Comments:
4. _____   Seeks interaction with students both in and out of the classroom. Comments:

Goal Five: Questioning Skills

1. _____   Uses questioning techniques that build higher level thinking skills. Comments:
2. _____   Requires students to go beyond recall. Comments:
3. _____   Demonstrates application, analysis, and synthesis of material through questioning. Comments:
4. _____   Uses motivating and divergent questions that synthesize learning. Comments:

(continued)

Goal Six: Becoming a Professional

1. _____ Making progress in reflecting on and improving their learning as a professional educator. Comments:
2. _____ Displays a positive attitude with students and faculty. Demonstrates enthusiasm for learning. Comments:
3. _____ Asks teachers how they would handle various problems in lessons and with classroom management. Comments:
4. _____ Beginning to become aware of what works, why it works, and what does not work. Seeks to change what doesn't. Comments:

Source: Reprinted with permission from the Ohio State University, College of Education, School of Teaching and Learning. Global Education Program.

Form #2
Student Teacher Observation and Conference Form

The observation of a student teacher serves as a tangible basis for discussion among the cooperating teacher, university supervisor, and student teacher.

Student Teacher: _____ Date: _____ Time _____

Subject:_____ Grade: _____ Cooperating School: _____

Cooperating Teacher: _____ University Supervisor:_____

Describe the student teacher's performance:

I.   Communication and Interaction Skills

II. Teaching Atmosphere and Management

III. Subject Matter, Knowledge, and Instruction

IV. Professional Attitudes

V. Assessment, Diagnosis, and Evaluation

Additional Comments:

Name: _____ Position : _____

Source: Bloomsburg University, Department of Curriculum and Foundations. *Student Teaching Handbook*, 1992.

Form #3
Student Teacher Final Evaluation Form

This FINAL EVALUATION FORM has been completed for the student teacher by the University Supervisor or the Cooperating Teacher named below. The narrative assessment and the ratings are a measure of student teaching competencies and are not intended to be a measure in comparison to experienced classroom teachers.

Candidate_____ Date_____ Fall/Spring 1/2 (circle)
      Last   Middle   First
Curriculum_____ Grade(s)_____ Subject_____
Narrative Evaluation:

Performance Evaluation Scale: 5--Superior; 4--Good, Above Average; 3--Acceptable, Average; 2--Weakness, Need to Improve; 1--Unsatisfactory

COMPETENCIES BY AREA:
I.   Communication and Interaction Skills
    A. English Usage--Oral   ____
    B. English Usage--Written   ____
    C. Presents Ideas Effectively ____
    D. Handwriting   ____
    E. Spelling   ____
    F. Voice   ____
    G. Promotes Interaction   ____
    H. Understands Nonverbal Cues ____

II. Teaching Atmosphere and Management
    A. Class Control   ____
    B. Attitude Toward Students   ____
    C. Pupil Responsiveness   ____
    D. Creates Positive Environment ____
    E. Instructional Strategies   ____
    F. Management Strategies   ____

(continued)

III. Subject Matter, Knowledge, and Instruction
    A. Mastery of Subject Matter ____
    B. Selection of Appropriate Goals ____
    C. Planning & Organizing Lessons ____
    D. Implementation of Lesson Plans ____
    E. Use of Media and Resources ____
    F. Degree of Flexibility ____
    G. Imagination and Creativity ____
    H. Applies Principles of Learning ____

IV. Professional Attitudes
    A. Interest in Self-Improvement ____
    B. Acceptance of Criticism ____
    C. Commitment to Teaching ____
    D. Dependability and Promptness ____
    E. Initiative ____
    F. Enthusiasm ____
    G. Poise and Self-Control ____
    H. Relationships with Colleagues ____
    I. Maintains Appropriate Records ____
    J. Dress and Grooming ____
       Comment:

V. Assessment, Diagnosis and Evaluation
    A. Student Developmental Needs ____
    B. Education Programs ____
    C. Curricular Materials ____
    D. Instructional Strategies ____
    E. Evaluation Methods & Materials ____
    F. Professional Role ____
    G. Community Expectations ____
    H. School System Expectations ____
    I. Acts Upon Feedback ____
    J. Evaluation of Student Learning ____

Name_____ Position_____
Office copy (white), Student copy (yellow), and Cooperating Teacher copy (pink)

Source: Bloomsburg University, Department of Curriculum and Foundations.
Student Teaching Handbook, 1992.

Form #4
Teacher Observation Form

___ Announced
___ Unannounced
___ Invited

Name _____ Date _____ Time _____

Number of Students _____ Room No. _____ Subject _____

Observer's Signature _____

Yes	No	N/A	I. Anticipatory Set	Narrative
			A. Were the students brought onto task quickly?	
			B. Were the students made aware of the objectives and their purposes?	
			C. Were the objectives at the correct level of difficulty?	
			D. Were the objectives related to past, present, or future objectives or purposes?	
			II. Instructional Input	
			A. Did the teacher give an adequate explanation of the learning before students were expected to put it into practice?	
			B. Did the teacher involve the students early and keep them involved throughout the lesson?	
			C. What strategies were used to get the learning across to the students? ___ Lecture ___ Group discussion ___ Inquiry___ Role playing ___ Student input ___ other	

(continued)

			D. Did the teacher model the learning and its application for the students?	
			E. What level of Bloom's taxonomy were observed? ___ Knowledge ___ Comprehension ___ Application ___ Analysis ___ Synthesis ___ Evaluation	
			III. Monitor and Adjust (create, observe, interpret, react to overt behavior.)	
			A. Did the teacher check regularly to make sure that all students understood the learning?	
			B. Did the teacher adjust the teaching to the student needs?	
			C. Was independent practice assigned only after students proved their ability to perform proficiently in guided practice?	
			D. Was homework assigned based on the day's learning?	
			IV. Closure	
			A. Was there a review at the end of the lesson?	
			B. Were the students involved in the closing activities?	
			V. Standards	
			A. Did the students seem to know what was expected of them in terms of behavior?	
			B. Were all materials and equipment necessary for the class on hand?	
			C. Was the period devoted primarily to the task of the day?	
			D. Was the classroom kept in good order?	

(continued)

			E. Were bulletin boards and displays effective and in good taste?	
			F. Did the teacher consistently apply moderately pleasant feeling tones?	
			Motivation, Reinforcement, Retention	
			A. What forms of motivation were used during class by the teacher? ___ Interest ___ Feeling tone ___ Success ___ Tension ___ Feedback to students	
			B. Did the teacher provide an adequate amount of original learning?	
			C. What methods were used to provide for positive transfer? ___ Similarity ___ Association ___ Critical elements ___ Degree of original learning	

Signature of teacher _____

Date _____

Source: Reprinted with the permission of the Bloomsburg School District. Bloomsburg, Pennsylvania.

Chapter 9

ॐ

Code of Ethics for Teachers

A teacher's ethical behavior is extremely important. In the *Dictionary of Philosophy*, A. R. Lacey (1976, p. 60) defined ethics as "an enquiry into how men ought to act in general, not as means to a given end." Lacey further explained that the primary notion in the concept include ought, obligation, duty, right, and wrong. First year teachers or student teachers are often confronted with this dilemma. They want to know behaviors that are considered as right or wrong. They want to know their duty in the school, what is expected of them, and what is considered a good performance. Student teachers always experience pressure to impress not only the cooperating teacher but also the school administration. It is advisable that early in the assignment, preferably during the first week, the student teacher contact the school principal for a copy of the school's rules of conduct that teachers are expected to follow. It should be remembered that student teachers are obliged to obey these rules of conduct just as full-time teachers do.

As a professional, a teacher represents several institutions as well as the teaching profession itself. While teachers primarily represent the school in which they are employed, their behavior also reflects upon their training institution. Therefore, a teacher indirectly represents the college or university that provided his or her teacher training.

Student teachers' behavior and professional attitude affect much more than their grade. During student teaching, the teacher training institution is directly responsible for the behavior of its student teachers. The continuation of agreements between teacher training institutions and cooperating schools often depends on the caliber of prospective teachers in the program. A student teacher's behavior reflects the integrity of his or her training institution and also contributes to a significant portion of the student teacher's overall grade for each teaching placement. Therefore, the demonstration of ethical behavior benefits both teacher training institutions and student teachers.

Ethical classroom behavior can be a useful tool for teachers and student teachers. It can limit classroom management problems, help establish a good rapport with students and colleagues, and contribute to an overall positive teaching atmosphere. Students will often learn from the teacher's example, and student behavior will be cued by an anticipated teacher response. Teacher behavior sets a standard for acceptable student behavior, and unethical behavior by the teacher may have a visible or intrinsic negative impact on students. Unethical teacher behavior may have other serious consequences as well.

Unethical behavior can result in termination of a teacher's contract or removal of a student teacher from the student teaching assignment. This chapter includes the National Education Association's (NEA's) code of ethics, which is helpful in determining which teacher behaviors may be seen as unethical. Furthermore, the following behaviors by student teachers could be considered unethical in many school districts across the nation:

1. Participating in faculty gossip that may concern school politics, antiadministration issues, or plans for a teachers' strike. Student teachers must not align themselves with any faction. They must endeavor to remain neutral at all times.
2. Sharing with parents information about other people's children. Teacher–parent conferences are a very critical aspect of teaching. During a teacher–parent conference, student teachers must focus on the particular student concerned.. It is unethical to mention something about one parent's child to another parent.

3. Using inappropriate language. Student teachers must avoid insensitive jokes that may be perceived as unprofessional by school administrators and teachers. If the joke was initiated by a teacher or administrator, the student teacher must avoid repeating the joke.

4. Gossiping in public. Student teachers as well as regular teachers must learn to leave all educational issues in the building. It is unprofessional to discuss school matters at social events such as at the bowling alley, football stadium, or movie theater.

5. Developing intimacy with students. Student teachers must maintain a professional distance from their students.

It is important to keep in mind that expectations for ethical teacher behavior extend well beyond classroom walls. Behaviors exerted outside of the classroom are often observed by the community as a whole. As the school is a functioning part of the community, the teacher must also act within community standards.

Acting in an ethical manner is usually a product of good judgment, responsibility, foresight, and patience. As role models, teachers must understand that their behavior sends a strong message to students. Teachers should avoid unethical behavior as well as all behaviors that are ethically questionable. Remember that teacher behavior will be judged by parents, students, faculty members, and administrators. Each of these groups may have varying opinions about what behavior is ethical.

The NEA's code of ethics is presented below. This code is usually adopted, in its entirety, by individual states. However, enforcement of the code is dependent on each state's Department of Education. In other words, each state creates different provisions for enforcement.

Code of Ethics of the Education Profession
Adopted by the NEA Representative Assembly, 1975*

Preamble

The educator, believing in the worth and dignity of each human being, recognizes the supreme importance of the pursuit of truth, devotion to excellence, and the nurture of democratic principles. Essential to these goals is the protection of freedom to learn and to teach and the guarantee of equal educational opportunity for all. The educator accepts the responsibility to adhere to the highest ethical standards.

The educator recognizes the magnitude of the responsibility inherent in the teaching process. The desire for the respect and confidence of one's colleagues, of students, of parents, and of the members of the community provides the incentive to attain and maintain the highest possible degree of ethical conduct. The Code of Ethics of the Education Profession *indicates the aspiration of all educators and provides standards by which to judge conduct.*

The remedies specified by the NEA and/or its affiliates for the violation of any provision of this Code *shall be exclusive and no such provision shall be enforceable in any form other than one specifically designated by the NEA or its affiliates.*

Principle I
Commitment to the Student

The educator strives to help each student realize his or her potential as a worthy and effective member of society. The educator therefore works to stimulate the spirit of inquiry, the acquisition of knowledge and understanding, and the thoughtful formulation of worthy goals.

In fulfillment of the obligation to the student, the educator —

1. Shall not unreasonably restrain the student from independent action in the pursuit of learning.
2. Shall not unreasonably deny the student access to varying points of view.
3. Shall not deliberately suppress or distort subject matter relevant to the student's progress.

4. Shall make reasonable effort to protect the student from conditions harmful to learning or to health and safety.

5. Shall not intentionally expose the student to embarrassment or disparagement.

6. Shall not on the basis of race; color; creed; sex; national origin; marital status; political or religious beliefs; family, social, or cultural background; or sexual orientation unfairly—

   a.) Exclude any student from participating in any program.

   b.) Deny benefits to any student.

   c.) Grant any advantage to any student.

7. Shall not use professional relationships with students for private advantage.

8. Shall not disclose information about students obtained in the course of professional service unless disclosure serves a compelling professional purpose or is required by law.

Principle II
Commitment to the Profession

The education profession is vested by the public with a trust and responsibility requiring the highest ideals of professional service.

In the belief that the quality of the services of the education profession directly influences the nation and its citizens, the educator shall exert every effort to raise professional standards, to promote a climate that encourages the exercise of professional judgment, to achieve conditions that attract persons worthy of the trust to careers in education, and to assist in preventing the practice of the profession by unqualified persons.

In fulfillment of the obligation to the profession, the educator —

1. Shall not in an application for a professional position deliberately make a false statement or fail to disclose a material fact related to competency and qualifications.

2. Shall not misrepresent his/her professional qualifications.

3. Shall not assist any entry into the profession of a person known to be unqualified in respect to character, education, or other relevant attribute.

4. Shall not knowingly make a false statement concerning the qualifications of a candidate for a professional position.
5. Shall not assist a noneducator in the unauthorized practice of teaching.
6. Shall not disclose information about colleagues obtained in the course of professional service unless disclosure serves a compelling professional purpose or is required by law.
7. Shall not knowingly make false or malicious statements about a colleague.
8. Shall not accept any gratuity, gift, or favor that might impair or appear to influence professional decisions or action.

*Reprinted by permission of the National Education Association, Washington, D.C.

Glossary

The following are terms frequently encountered by educators. Although some terms may seem self-explanatory, this list was compiled from requests by education majors and student teachers.

Ability grouping: assigning pupils to homogenous groups according to their intellectual ability for instruction.

Academic learning time (ALT): amount of academic instruction time during which students are actively and successfully engaged in the learning process.

Academic support: expenditures for the support services that are an integral part of an educational institution's primary mission.

Accelerated program: more rapid advancement of superior students through the different levels (grades) of a school.

Advanced placement: programs provided by high schools, in cooperation with community colleges or universities, in which qualifying students take college-level courses and receive college credits for their work.

Affective learning: acquisition of feelings, senses, emotions, will, and other aspects of social and psychological development gained through feeling rather than through intellectualization.

Alternative education: unconventional educational experiences for students who are inadequately taught in regular classes. Alternatives include schools without walls, street academies, free schools, and second-chance schools.

Anticipatory set: a term used to indicate the need to plan an introductory activity that will capture students' attention, help them see the purpose and value of what is to be learned, and relate what is to be learned to what they already know.

Applied behavioral analysis (ABA): based on the principles of B. F. Skinner's operant conditioning. Teachers reward or reinforce learners when they correctly answer a question, perform a task, or learn a new skill.

Assessment: process of collecting, synthesizing, and interpreting information to aid in decision making or evaluation.

At-risk students: students in danger of failing to complete their education with the skills necessary to survive in modern society.

Attention deficit disorder (ADD): learning disability where students become hyperactive, restless, and experience difficulty focusing on learning tasks.

Behavior disorders: conduct disorders, anxiety-withdrawal disorders, lack of self-control, hyperactivity, and immaturity.

Behavior modification: conscious attempt to change behavior through clinical use of hypnosis, drug therapy, or electroconvulsive shock treatment.

Behavioral objective: precise statement of what the learner must do to demonstrate mastery at the end of a prescribed learning task.

Behaviorism: a psychological and educational theory that contends that behavior represents the essence of a person. Behaviorists contend that behavior can be explained as a response to stimuli.

Brainstorming: an instructional alternative where a period of time is given to learners before an activity or assignment to withhold judgment or criticism while they produce a large number of ways to do something such as resolve a problem.

Classroom management: a multifaceted dimension of teaching that includes the content, method, and values that infuse the classroom environment; planning; and discipline practices.

Closure: a form of review that concludes a lesson by having students recall all major points discussed in the course of the lecture or class period.

Code of ethics: formal statement of appropriate professional behaviors.

Cognitive development: a learner's acquisition of facts, concepts, and principles through intellectualization.

Cognitive domain: area of learning that involves the acquisition and use of knowledge.

College supervisor: a staff member of a teacher-education institution who has responsibility for supervision of student teachers and the conditions under which they carry on their work.

Content: subject matter.

Convergent learning: learning in which there is one answer to be learned.

Cooperating school: a school in which student teachers engage in professional experiences, but which is not administered by, staffed by, or under the jurisdiction of the teacher training institution.

Cooperating teacher (coop): a teacher in a cooperating school under whose guidance and supervision prospective teachers engage in professional experiences.

Cooperative learning: a term which refers to teaching strategies used for group instruction or peer tutoring. Cooperative learning involves students working together, usually in mixed-ability groups. A four-person team (group), for example, would consist of the highest achiever, the lowest achiever, and two average or mid-level achievers. A second group would be made up of the second highest achiever, the next to the lowest achiever, and two in the middle. In putting together a cooperative learning group, consideration must be given to ensuring a balance of genders, ethnicities, and backgrounds.

Core curriculum: a student-centered organizational emphasis that combines broad areas of academic disciplines into manageable instructional units such as social studies and language arts for integration in learning.

Criterion-referenced scores: scores of a student compared to specific preestablished standards or criteria.

Curriculum: all educational experiences provided by a particular school district.

Deductive reasoning: a system of learning that begins with "first principles" or generalizations and arrives at "secondary principles" or specifics.

Direct instruction (expository teaching): occurs when teachers control instruction by presenting information, giving directions to the class, and using criticism; associated with teacher-centered, teacher-controlled classrooms; an instructional procedure for teaching content in the most efficient, straightforward way.

Director of student teaching: the college staff member who is the supervisory or administrative head of teacher education work done in laboratory schools or in cooperating schools.

Discipline: the treatment of misbehavior in classrooms and schools.

Divergent thinking: an open-ended type of thinking that extends in different directions and considers multiple answers or solutions to a problem.

Early-childhood education: the education children receive in a recognized institution before they start kindergarten.

Education for All Handicapped Children Act (Public Law 94-142): law requiring handicapped students to be placed in the least restrictive, that is, the most normal, school environment they can succeed in.

Effective teaching: a movement to improve teaching performance based on the outcomes of educational research.

English as a second language (ESL): a component of virtually all bilingual educational programs in the United States that is designed to help instruct students whose primary language is not English.

Exceptional learners: a classification used to describe handicapped and gifted learners.

Executive officer for teacher education: the person directly in charge of the teacher education program of a teacher training institution.

Feedback: knowledge that teachers provide students to inform them of their progress and to help them learn to monitor themselves and improve their own learning.

Formative assessment: refers to ongoing student assessment conducted during the course of instruction.

Full inclusion: a term to refer to the assumption that instructional practices and technological supports are presently available to accommodate all students in the schools and classrooms they would normally attend if not disabled (Rogers, 1993).

Gifted and Talented Act (Public Law 95-561): provides federal funding for gifted education.

Gifted learner: term most frequently applied to those with exceptional intellectual ability; it may also refer to learners with outstanding ability in athletics, leadership, artistic creativity, and so forth.

Head Start Program: a federally funded preschool program for economically disadvantaged three- and four-year-old children, intended to counteract negative environmental effects.

Heterogeneous grouping: a group or class of students who show normal variation in ability or performance.

Homogeneous grouping: classification of pupils for the purpose of forming an instructional group with a high degree of similarity in certain factors that affect learning.

Hyperactivity: behavior disorder characterized by abnormal amounts of movement, off-task behavior, and restlessness.

Inclusion: a term to refer to efforts to educate each child, to the maximum extent appropriate, in the school and classroom he or she would otherwise attend. It involves bringing support services to the child, rather than moving the child to the services, and requires only that the child benefit from being in the class, rather than keep up with the other students (Rogers, 1993).

Individualized educational program (IEP): mechanism through which a handicapped child's special needs are identified; goals, objectives, and services are outlined; and methods for evaluating progress are delineated.

Individualized instruction: instructional maneuvers that attempt to tailor teaching and learning to a learner's unique strengths and needs.

Inquiry: a process of asking questions and conducting a thorough scientific investigation.

Integration: mixing students of different races and ethnic backgrounds in schools to overcome segregation.

Knowledge base: a term which refers to the foundation upon which professional education programs are built.

Laboratory school: a school largely or entirely under the control of a teacher-preparing institution located on or near the campus, and organized with staff and facilities for the specific purpose of preparing teachers.

Latchkey children: children between 6 and 13 years of age who do not have adult supervision for some part of the day.

Learning: a change in behavior as a result of experience.

Learning disability: an educationally significant discrepancy between a child's apparent capacity for language behavior and his or her actual level of language functioning.

Learning modules: form of individualized instruction whereby students use self-contained learning activities that guide them to know or to be able to do something.

Learning resource center: a specially designed space containing a wide range of supplies and equipment for use by individual students and small groups pursuing independent study.

Learning styles: the cognitive, affective, and physiological traits of learner as they interact in the classroom environment. Basically, learning style includes how individuals learn best; their learning personality; and their tendency to use different sensory modes (visual, auditory, kinesthetic) to understand experiences and to learn.

Mainstreaming: a term generally used to mean the selective placement of special education students in one or more "regular" education classes (Rogers, 1993).

Motivation: impetus that causes one to act.

Multicultural education: an environment whereby the school gives educational emphasis to culture and how it influences the teaching and learning process.

Multiculturalism: an environment of multiple cultures working together with mutual respect.

Multiethnic education: educational practices that encourage learners to revere both their roots and culture, as well as the culture and diversity of others.

Objective: a purpose or a goal.

Objective test: a test yielding results that can be evaluated or scored with like outcomes by different people.

Observation: professional experiences in which prospective teachers see and analyze teaching and learning.

Observation techniques: structured methods for observing various aspects of the entire school or specific classroom environments.

Outcome-based education (OBE): an education program that emphasizes general learning outcomes rather than specific content to be covered. Every student is expected to meet a school's learning outcomes.

Participation: professional experiences in which the prospective teacher, under supervision, assumes an active part in teaching students. Participation includes activities along a continuum between observation and full responsibility for teaching or directing the activities of a group in a school or other community agency.

Professional laboratory or clinical experiences: an all-inclusive term for any supervised contact with children, youths, and adults (through observation, participation, and teaching) that makes a direct contribution to prospective teachers' understanding of the teaching and learning process.

Programmed instruction (PI): instruction whereby material to be learned usually is presented in small steps (called frames) so students can teach themselves. Learners respond to information, and if the response is correct they are given positive reinforcement and the next step or frame is presented.

Public Law 93-247: defines abuse and neglect as "physical or mental injury, sexual abuse, negligent treatment, or maltreatment of a child under 18 by a person who is responsible for the child's welfare under circumstances which indicate that the child's health or welfare is harmed or threatened thereby."

Public Law 94-142 (Education for All Handicapped Children Act): requires handicapped students to be placed in the least restrictive (most normal) school environment.

Public Law 95-561 (Gifted and Talented Act): provides federal funding for gifted education.

Questioning frequency: the number of questions teachers ask during learning activities.

Regular education initiative: the discussion of either the merger of the administration of special and "regular" education or the merger of the funding stream of each.

Role playing: learners take on the role of another person to see what it would be like to be that person.

Rote learning: a form of learning that emphasizes memorizing specific items of information rather than exploring relationships among topics.

Simulation: a method of instruction that attempts to create circumstances analogous to real-life situations.

Standardized test: an instrument presenting a uniform task or series of tasks to be performed according to specified directions and under uniform conditions so that individual performances may be compared with one another and with a reference or normative group.

Structured observations: judgments or impressions conducted according to a predetermined plan.

Student-centered curriculum: a curriculum organization in which learning activities are centered on the interests of the pupils in the class.

Student teacher: a prospective teacher engaged in a student teaching field experience.

Student teaching: guided teaching in which the prospective teacher, over a period of consecutive weeks, is involved in the development and direction of teaching and learning activities applicable to a learner group.

Student teaching field experience: the total design under which student teachers observe, participate, and teach under the direct supervision of a cooperating teacher or supervising teacher. (Also referred to as the "student teaching program.")

Student teams achievement division (STAD): a cooperative learning strategy designed to teach basic facts, concepts, and skills through the use of multiability learning teams.

Subject-centered curriculum: a curriculum organization in which learning activities and content are planned around subject fields of knowledge, such as history and science.

Subjective test: a test that will not necessarily have the same outcome when scored by different persons.

Supervising teacher: a teacher in a laboratory school in whose classes prospective teachers engage in professional laboratory experiences.

Taxonomies: classification of learning levels or thinking levels into an organized scheme. Some are hierarchical (like Benjamin Bloom's).

Teacher certification: process whereby each state determines the requirements for obtaining a license to teach, processes applications, and issues such licenses.

Teacher effectiveness training (TET): program developed to encourage teachers to establish open and honest communication in the classroom using such techniques as active listening and conflict resolution.

Teacher role: the set of behaviors that is generally expected of one who occupies a teaching position.

Teaching styles: clusters of teaching tactics regarding learning and classroom management that are based on different philosophies and psychology.

Team teaching: a plan by which several teachers, organized into a team with a leader, provide instruction for a larger group of children than would usually be found in a self-contained classroom.

Time on task: time when students are actively engaged in academic tasks.

Time-out: reducing unwanted student behavior by removing a disobedient student from a situation and from the attention and rewards that situation yields.

Tracking: a method of placing students according to their ability level in homogeneous classes or learning experiences where they all follow the same curriculum, e.g., college preparatory or vocational.

Values clarification: a model, composed of various strategies, that encourages students to express and clarify their values on different topics.

Wait time: the period of silence both before and after a student responds.

Warmth: teachers' abilities to demonstrate that they care for students as people.

With-it-ness: ability of a teacher to communicate to students that the teacher is aware of student behavior throughout the classroom at all times even when the teacher is not looking directly at the students.

References and Bibliography

Andrews, L. O. 1964. *Student Teaching*. New York: Center for Applied Research in Education.

Banks, James A. 1976. "Multicultural Education." In *Multicultural Education: Goals, Teaching Strategies, and Evaluations* edited by the Association for Supervision and Curriculum Development. Washington, D.C. Videotape.

Banks, James A., and Cherry A. McGee Banks. 1997. *Multicultural Education: Issues and Perspectives*. 3rd ed. Boston: Allyn and Bacon.

Bloomsburg University. 1992. *Student Teaching Evaluation, Values and Descriptions*. Bloomsburg, Pa.: Bloomsburg University, Department of Curriculum and Foundations.

Bullough, Robert V., Jr. 1989. *First Year Teacher: A Case Study*. New York: Columbia University, Teachers College.

Cangelosi, James S. 1993. *Classroom Management Strategies: Gaining and Maintaining Students' Cooperation*. 2nd ed. New York: Longman.

Canter, Lee, and Marlene Canter. 1988. *Assertive Discipline: A Take-Charge Approach for Today's Educator*. Los Angeles: Canter and Associates.

———. 1992. *Assertive Discipline: Positive Behavior Management for Today's Classroom*. Santa Monica, Calif.: Canter and Associates.

Corcoran, E. 1981. "Position Shock: The Beginning Teacher's Paradox." *The Journal of Teacher Education* 32: 19–23.

Cruickshank, Donald R., Deborah Bainer, and Kim Metcalf. 1995. *The Act of Teaching*. New York: McGraw-Hill.

Derman-Sparks, L. 1995. "Children and Diversity." *Early Childhood Today* 10(3): 42–45.

Eggen, Paul D., and Donald P. Kauchak. 1996. *Strategies for Teachers: Teaching Content and Thinking Skills*. Boston: Allyn and Bacon.

Farris, Pamela J. 1996. *Teaching, Bearing the Torch*. Madison, Wis.: Brown and Benchmark.

Fleming, Maria, Gabrielle Lyon, Ting-Yi Oei, Rosa Hernandez Sheets, Glenda Valentine, and Elsie Williams, eds. 1998. *Starting Small: Teaching Tolerance in Preschool and Early Grades*. Montgomery, Ala.: Southern Poverty Law Center.

Fogerty, Robin, ed. 1998. *Block Scheduling: A Video tape and collection of articles*. Bloomington, Indiana: Phi Delta Kappa International.

Fuller, F. F., and O. H. Brown. 1975. "Becoming a Teacher." In K. Ryan (Ed.), *Teacher Education. Seventy-fourth Yearbook of the National Society of Education*. Chicago: University of Chicago Press.

Glasser, William. 1965. *Reality Therapy*. New York: Harper and Row.

———. 1986. *Control Theory in the Classroom*. New York: Harper and Row.

Hewit, J. Scott, and Kathleen S. Whittier. 1997. *Teaching Methods for Today's School: Collaboration and Inclusion*. Boston: Allyn and Bacon.

Hodgkinson, Harold. 1991. "Reform Versus Reality." *Phi Delta Kappan*, September 1991, pp. 9-16 in *Education*, Annual Editions 1993/94, pp. 36-42.

Johnson, James A., Victor Dupuis, Diann Musial, and Gene Hall. 1994. *Introduction to the Foundations of American Education*. 9th ed. Boston: Allyn and Bacon.

Klein, Jennifer L. 1998. "Lesson Planning in the Block Schedule" *Journal for the Pennsylvania Council for the Social Studies*, vol.4, Summer, pp. 28-32

Kounin, Jacob S. 1970. *Discipline and Group Management in Classrooms*. New York: Holt, Rinehart & Winston.

Kounin, Jacob S., and Paul V. Gump. 1959. "The Ripple Effect in Discipline." *Educational Digest* 24: 43–45.

Lacey, A. R. 1976. *A Dictionary of Philosophy*. London: Routledge and Kegan Paul.

Morganett, Lee. 1995. "Ten Tips for Improving Teacher-Student Relationships." *Social Education* 59(1): 27–28.

National Education Association. 1996. *Handbook 1996–1997*. Washington, D.C.: National Education Association.

Ohio State University. 1988. *Student Teaching Handbook*. Columbus, Ohio: Ohio State University, College of Education.

Orlich, Donald C., Richard C. Callahan, Harry W. Gibson, Robert J. Harder, Donald P. Kauchak, Andrew J. Keogh, and R. A. Pendergrass. 1994. *Teaching Strategies: A Guide to Better Instruction*. 4th ed. Lexington, Mass.: D.C. Heath and Company.

Orlich, Donald C., Robert J. Harder, Richard C. Callahan, and Harry W. Gibson. 1998. *Teaching Strategies: A Guide to Better Instruction*. 5th ed. Boston: Houghton Mifflin.

Osunde, Egerton O. 1996. The Effect on Student Teachers on the Teaching Behavior of Cooperating Teachers. *Education*, vol. 116, no. 4. pp. 612-618.

Pang, Valerie Ooka. 1994. "Why Do We Need This Class: Multicultural Education for Teachers." *Phi Delta Kappan*, vol. 76, no. 4, December, p. 289-293.

Rogers, Joy. 1993. "The Inclusion Revolution." *Research Bulletin*, Phi Delta Kappa Center for Evaluation, Development, and Research, No. 11, May, pp. 1-6.

Sapon-Shevin, M. 1983. "Teaching Children About Differences: Resources for Teaching." *Young Children* 38(2): 24–32.

Schmidt, Mary W., and Nancy E. Harriman, 1998. *Teaching Strategies for Inclusive Classrooms: Schools, Students, Strategies, and Success.* Fort Worth, Tex.: Harcourt Brace.

Sheets, Rosa Hernandez. 1997. "Reflection #9: The Inclusive Classroom." In Maria Fleming et al. (Eds.), *Starting Small: Teaching Tolerance in Preschool and Early Grades.* Montgomery, Ala.: Southern Poverty Law Center.

Shulman, L. S. 1986. "Paradigms and Research Programs in the Study of Teaching: A Contemporary Perspective." In *Handbook of Research on Teaching*, edited by Merlin C. Wittrock. 3rd ed. New York: Macmillan.

Skinner, B. F. 1953. *Science and Human Behavior.* New York: Macmillan.

———. 1954. "The Science of Learning and the Art of Teaching." *Harvard Educational Review* 24: 86–97.

Slavin, Robert E. 1992. "Cooperative Learning in Social Studies: Balancing the Social and the Studies." In *Cooperative Learning in the Social Studies Classroom.* Washington, D.C.: National Council for the Social Studies.

Statistical Abstract of the United States, 1990. Washington, D.C.: U.S. Government Printing Office, 1989.

Sullivan, Richard, and Jerry L. Wircenski. 1988. "Fifty Tips on Motivating Students." *Vocational Education Journal*, vol. 63, no. 5, p. 39-40, August 1988.

Teaching in the Block: Strategies for Engaging Active learners, edited by Robert L. Canady and Michael D. Rettig. Princeton, N.J: Eye on Education, 320p. 1996.

Veenman, S. 1984. "Perceived Problems of Beginning Teachers." *Review of Educational Research* 54(2): 143–178.

Wallen, Carl J. 1968, January. *Establishing Teaching Principles in the Area of Classroom Management* (Interim Report, Project No. 5-0916). Monmouth, Oreg.: Teaching Research. Appendix A, p. 15.

Zeichner, K. M. 1986. "Teacher Socialization Research and the Practice of Teaching." *Education and Society* 3: 25–37.

Index